HITLER
VERSUS
STALIN

THIS IS A CARLTON BOOK

Design copyright © 2001 Carlton Publishing Group
Text copyright © 2001 Professor John Erickson

This edition published in 2004 by Carlton Books Ltd
A Division of the Carlton Publishing Group
20 Mortimer Street, London W1T 3JW

A CIP catalogue for this book is available from the British Library.

ISBN 1-84442-727-7

Picture Research: Sergei Kudryashov
Executive Editor: Sarah Larter
Editors: Paul Doherty, Janice Anderson
Art Editor: Peter Bailey
Design: Simon Mercer
Picture Manager: Sally Claxton
Production: Garry Lewis
Jacket Design: Alison Tutton

Printed in Dubai

HITLER
VERSUS
STALIN

THE SECOND WORLD WAR ON THE EASTERN FRONT IN PHOTOGRAPHS

PROFESSOR JOHN & LJUBICA ERICKSON

CARLTON
BOOKS

CONTENTS

FOREWORD

On Sunday morning 22 June 1941, Adolf Hitler launched the greatest land campaign in world history: Operation *Barbarossa*, the invasion of the Soviet Union. This was total war without match, stupefying in its dimension, horrendous in its cruelty, harrowing in its degradation. Hitler committed his armies to a war of subjugation, to an ideological crusade against "Jewish-Bolshevism" and to racial war against Slav "subhumans".

In the course of "The Great Patriotic War 1941–1945", the Soviet Union mobilized 29,574,900 men. Wartime turnover in manpower amounted to 21,700,000. During 1,418 days of barbarized warfare, bereft of any legal or moral constraints, the Red Army's battlefield losses were more than half those 21 million, 11,440,100 men put permanently out of action. Almost one million men were variously convicted: 376,300 charged with desertion and 422,700 sentenced to service in penal battalions, or *strafbats*, assigned to the most dangerous sectors.

Civilians were not spared. German rule in occupied territory took the lives of some 16,350,000 citizens, shot, starved, neglected, or murdered in concentration camps. More than two million were deported for slave labour in the Reich. Soviet soldiers and civilians shared a combined death toll of 27–28 million souls. Each minute of this war cost 9–10 lives, each hour 587, each day 14,000. Savage partisan warfare and ferocious German retribution compounded the horrors.

Huge hunks of fronts disintegrated. Entire armies vanished, some to reappear later, others with fatal damage. Between 1941 and 1943, the Wehrmacht destroyed almost a third of 570 Soviet rifle divisions. The Red Army finally destroyed, disabled or captured 607 Axis divisions, at great cost to itself in men and machines: 96,500 tanks, 106,400 aircraft and 317,000 guns. Anglo-American armies fighting in North Africa, Italy and Western Europe destroyed 176 enemy divisions.

What Boris Pasternak called the "naked power of evil" had been unleashed. The cost to perpetrator and victim of first suppressing and then exorcising it was visited on the wartime generation and also on their descendants, mindful of inconsolable grief and ineluctable sorrows.

John Erickson   Ljubica Erickson

1939-1941

DANGEROUS DECEPTIONS

"Let them come. We are ready."

J. V. STALIN

On the morrow of the signing of the Treaty of Non-Aggression between Germany and the Soviet Union, the notorious Nazi-Soviet Pact of 23 August 1939, Stalin declared himself well pleased. He had not only outwitted Adolf Hitler, he had also deceived him for the time being. The Soviet Union could now dictate the fate of the Baltic states, Finland, Bessarabia and Bukovina, and immediate territorial gain was guaranteed when the Red Army invaded Poland's eastern provinces on 17 September 1939. With the prospect of further acquisitions, notably access to the Baltic, substantially improving the Soviet Union's strategic situation, Stalin could comfortably sit out the Second World War, finally exploiting the mutual exhaustion of the combatants while the Soviet Union remained unscathed and inviolate.

Deceit and delusion fed on each other. The Soviet "security circle" had apparently been squared. Contrived "neutralism" spared the Soviet Union the strain of general war. Secret territorial agreements enabled Stalin to recover Russia's former strategic frontiers. Yet Stalin's search for security led him inevitably toward territorial aggrandizement, steadily encroaching upon Germany's sphere of influence. During the winter of 1939–1940, Stalin waged war on Finland to seal off the

eastern Baltic. Soviet military performance was dismal, the cost 391,000 men killed, missing or wounded. The Red Army failed to pass rudimentary tests of military effectiveness. Marshal Kliment Voroshilov might boast "Comrades, our army is invincible", but this humiliation served only to encourage the German command and others to dismiss the Red Army as a serious force.

Stalin's delusion was abruptly shattered in June 1940 by the fall of France and the Wehrmacht's triumph in western Europe. Stalin cursed the English and the French for succumbing so easily. Hitler would now inevitably and irrevocably turn east. Stalin's frantic response was to launch the Red Army into the Baltic states in the north and Bessarabia and the Northern Bukovina in the south, exercising the territorial options concealed in the secret protocols to the 1939 Pact.

Paradoxically, the farther west and southwest Soviet frontiers were pushed, the more "security" appeared to diminish. Existing mobilization plans were rendered obsolete at a stroke. On the home front, industry went over to a virtual war footing. Strict controls were imposed on the Soviet work force and absenteeism was made punishable. The Red Army was subject to drastic disciplinary codes. The existing Soviet war plan dating back to 1938 was now hurriedly reviewed. Much to Stalin's displeasure, this initial review repeated the findings of the 1938 plan, that any major German offensive would develop to the north of the Pripet marshes. Together with Defence Commissar Semen Timoshenko, Stalin demanded an immediate revision of this review in order to pursue his conviction that the main attack would develop from the southwest, aimed directly at Kiev and the Ukraine. Stalin argued that in order to sustain protracted war, Hitler needed Ukrainian grain and Donbas coal. Accordingly, at Stalin's insistence, the new war plan assigned priority to the southwestern theatre. Here the Red Army proceeded to reinforce continuously and substantially, the origin of the ill-conceived, inappropriate deployments that were to take place on the eve of June 1941.

On 12 November 1940, the Soviet Foreign Minister Molotov met Hitler in Berlin. Molotov spurned German suggestions that the Soviet Union associate itself with the Axis in the Tripartite Pact. Stalin was more concerned about German encroachments in the Balkans, demanding assurances, guaranties and concessions. Hitler was incensed at Stalin's attitude, denouncing him as "a cold-blooded blackmailer". The Nazi–Soviet Pact was rapidly coming apart at the seams. Losing all interest in negotiation, one month and six days later, on 18 December 1940, Hitler issued Directive No. 21: "The German Armed Forces must be prepared *to crush Russia in a quick campaign* (Operation *Barbarossa*) even before the conclusion of war against England." Hitler was bent on war, Stalin committed to avoiding it at all costs.

As early as January 1941, Soviet intelligence received information on Hitler's intentions and German troop movements eastward. The Red Army set about reorganizing and rearming, unfortunately in haphazard fashion. Impressed by what the German Panzers had achieved in the west, Stalin abruptly ordered the reconstitution of disbanded tank and mechanized corps. The "class of 1940", generals and admirals newly promoted by Stalin, were sent back to school. Secret strategic war games that took place in January 1941 tested the revised war plan. The primacy of the southwestern theatre was confirmed, but the idea of a German surprise attack never entered the planners' heads. The obsession with a German strike into the Ukraine persisted. Frontier battles would last 10–15 days, by which time both the Wehrmacht and the Red Army would have concentrated and deployed. The Red Army would first defend, then launch its own retaliatory blow, carrying the war into enemy territory. As one senior Soviet commander observed much later, it was as if the Soviet Union was preparing for the war of 1914, not 1941.

General Georgii Zhukov's updated war plan submitted in mid-March 1941 simply restated these ideas against the background of intensified German military traffic eastward reported by Soviet intelli-

gence. The Wehrmacht dug deeper into the Balkans, entrenching itself in Hungary, Rumania and Bulgaria, closing in on Russia. In April 1941, Hitler invaded Yugoslavia and swept into Greece. Stalin flinched but barely reacted, confining himself merely to a futile, tardy gesture toward Yugoslavia. He was warned that Germany intended to attack, the target now Russia, the timing June. The effect of this and other warnings seemed only to stiffen Stalin's determination to avoid war with Germany, come what may. Deliberate signals were sent, confirming adherence to the 1939 Pact. Stalin even used the signing of the Neutrality Pact with Japan on 13 April to affirm friendship with Germany "in any event".

In May 1941, evidence of war intensified. Soviet agents in Germany confirmed German military preparations but added a fatal qualification that war would be preceded by a German ultimatum. This only encouraged Stalin's policy of appeasement, though on 5 May he acknowledged a "danger period" lasting until mid-summer. Thereafter, war might be deferred to 1942. The same day, the dam burst. The strategy of war-avoidance suffered a shattering blow. Red Army military intelligence reported, accurately, the concentration of 103–107 German divisions, including 12 Panzer divisions, aimed at the Soviet Union. The execution of the long-manifest threat seemed imminent.

The moment of truth had arrived for the Soviet General Staff. The Red Army must either launch a Soviet version of the *Blitzkrieg* or implement general mobilization. General Zhukov's plan of 15 May 1941 proposed using 152 Soviet divisions to destroy 100 German divisions. Stalin dismissed this as a recipe for disaster, forbidding either an offensive or mobilization. Hobbled by Stalin, the Red Army could neither attack nor defend. But fresh phantoms had come to haunt the Soviet leader. On 10 May 1941, Rudolf Hess, Hitler's deputy, made his extraordinary flight to Scotland. The upshot was to deflect Stalin's attention from the German threat and fix it upon a possible British anti-Soviet conspiracy. Previous British warnings about the consequences of settling with Germany he now interpreted as a sinister threat. Did Hess's arrival signal an Anglo–German deal to give Germany a free hand in the east, or yet another British manoeuvre to embroil him in war? Deliberate disinformation by British intelligence, exploiting Hess's flight, only succeeded in confirming Stalin's worst fears of a conspiracy.

The political strategy of "war-avoidance" and the military's approach to "creeping up on war" played havoc with Soviet defence preparations. Zigzag propaganda alternately reassured and unnerved the population, and confused the army. Mobilization planning – MP-41 – proceeded only in fits and starts. By June 1941, revised plans remained incomplete and timetables slipped disastrously. Plans at military district were unfinished and no plan existed to bring all forces to full readiness. The General Staff "Plan for the defence of the state frontiers" outlined deployments but lacked specific operational orders. The organization of frontier defence presumed that the Red Army would not be taken by surprise, that any decisive action would be preceded by a declaration of war and that initial enemy operations would involve only limited forces, giving the Red Army time to cover mobilization. Conscious that general mobilization had triggered war in 1914, Stalin not only ruled out mobilization but also withheld authorization to increase unit readiness lest this "provocation" provided Germany with a pretext to strike. His only concession was to agree to "covert mobilization" by calling up reservists in the guise of summer manoeuvres.

Soviet diplomacy dropped persistent hints that "a fresh compromise" with Berlin was possible and even in the offing. Economic supplies to Germany transported along the Trans–Siberian Railway from the Soviet Far East were speeded up. Berlin calculated that it could make economic demands on Russia exceeding the January 1941 trade agreement. It was this factor that persuaded many, the British intelligence included, to view German troop concentrations as pressure to wring further Soviet concessions. Moreover, Stalin could not persuade himself that Hitler would abandon that fundamental German strategic precept: never wage war on two fronts. Berlin hinted that negotiations might just be possible.

On 14 June 1941, Stalin authorized a Soviet press statement, discounting the imminence of war, denouncing rumours of a German attack as "completely without foundation", *provokatsiya* spread by "false friends". "The recent movement of German troops who have completed their operations in the Balkans are connected, it must be supposed, with other motives that have nothing to do with Soviet–German relations." The same day, the German High Command issued a warning order to German commands in the east, allocating the code word "Dortmund"

for the launch of Operation *Barbarossa*. All German preparations were to be completed by 15 June 1941.

Stalin waited in vain for a response from Berlin. The German command duly confirmed code words on 15 June, fixing the time and place of the German attack as "B-Day, Y-hours" (22 June 1941, 0300 hours), final dispositions to proceed after 18 June. Panzer divisions would move to their start lines by night. Desperately troubled Soviet front-line commanders telephoned Moscow only to be told: "There will be no war". This was precisely the burden of the report submitted to Stalin by Lavrenti Beria, head of the NKVD, on Saturday 21 June. Even as the Soviet military reported the first German movements, as the Luftwaffe was launching its aerial massacre of Soviet aircraft neatly parked on their airfields, Stalin refused to abandon his obsession with "provocations", in this instance German officers on an insubordinate personal rampage. Marshal Timoshenko could not persuade him that this was all-out war. Stalin forbade General Zhukov to activate defensive plans. Soviet forces were forbidden to cross German lines "with the sole exception of the air force", just as his air force was being destroyed on the ground. The Wehrmacht was already advancing into Russia, dive-bombers roaring ahead. Soviet soldiers watched German aircraft returning from bombing their rear.

At 4am in Berlin Foreign Minister Ribbentrop presented the Soviet Ambassador, Vladimir Dekanozov, with reasons for Germany taking "military counter-measures". Soviet Embassy telephones had been disconnected. Desperate for news, Embassy staff tuned in Moscow Radio for the 6am (Moscow time) news. To their astonishment, the news, preceded by a physical programme instruction and an item for children, reported only non-Soviet war news and progress in Soviet agriculture and industry.

"Hitler surely does not know about this." Stalin's desperate comment betrayed his utter disbelief that this could be war, not simply more intimidation to extract further concessions. War without ultimatum, without diplomatic preamble, without pretext, without a formal declaration was base deception, now denounced by the man who 22 months ago had prided himself on hoodwinking Hitler.

Stalin left it to Molotov to broadcast the state of war at noon on Sunday 22 June.

UNHOLY ALLIANCE

The conclusion of the German-Soviet Non-Aggression Treaty of 23 August 1939, commonly known as the "Nazi–Soviet Pact", stunned the world. It represented the most dramatic about-turn in diplomatic history. Just as Europe was about to go to war, these two states – known for their mutual hostility – pledged neutrality, non-aggression and mutual consultation. Attached to the published treaty was a secret protocol prescribing demarcated Soviet-German "spheres of influence". Stalin signalled his abandonment of collective security for reliance on neutrality. In effect, the Soviet Union promised neutrality in Hitler's war with the west in return for a German undertaking to stay away from Finland, Estonia, Latvia and eastern Poland.

Above
German Foreign Minister Joachim von Ribbentrop signs the German–Soviet Non-Aggression Pact. His trip to Moscow was announced on 21 August 1939. He arrived on 23 August. Negotiations were conducted between Ribbentrop, Vyacheslav Molotov and Joseph Stalin. The conclusion of a non-aggression treaty and a "secret additional protocol" was agreed.

Below
Stalin and Ribbentrop shake hands. Stalin: "The Soviet Government takes the Pact very seriously. I can guarantee on my word of honour that the Soviet Union would not betray its partner." That proved to be precisely the case, only it was not to be reciprocated.

DIVIDING THE SPOILS

At 3 a.m. on 17 September 1939, the Polish Ambassador in Moscow learned that the Soviet government had ordered the Red Army to cross the Polish frontier. Poland was caught in a horrendous trap, the Wehrmacht attacking from the west, the Red Army advancing from the east. The Polish command ordered that no resistance be offered to Soviet troops.

German troops had crossed the Bug river and besieged Brest, violating the agreed Soviet–German demarcation line. Colonel S. M. Krivoshein, 29th Light Tank Brigade, negotiated German withdrawal from Brest with Panzer General Heinz Guderian. In the Lvov area, German and Soviet troops "exchanged positions".

Left
Soviet and German troops meet. At 5.40 a.m. on 17 September 1939 Red Army cavalry and tanks crossed the Soviet–Polish frontier line. Stalin had requested that German aircraft should not fly east of the Bialystok–Brest Litovsk–Lvov line in order to avoid incidents. The next day Stalin expressed "certain doubts" as to whether the German High Command would honour the Moscow agreements and the agreed demarcation lines.

Right
Colonel General Heinz Guderian (centre) and Colonel Semen Krivoshein (on Guderian's left) at a farewell parade of Soviet and German troops with salutes to both flags, marking the hand-over of the fortress of Brest to the Russians. The Bug river marked the demarcation line; the German army had to evacuate territory east of this boundary.

Above
Hardly a rapturous reception for the entry of Soviet troops into the Polish city of Lwów (Lvov). German troops withdrew on 21–22 September in line with the "exchange of positions". There was a strong Polish potential to defend the city against the Red Army but the city commandant General Langner submitted to persistent Soviet demands and, after negotiations, surrendered.

"FRIENDS FALL OUT": MOLOTOV IN BERLIN

Soviet Foreign Minister Molotov arrived in Berlin on 12 November 1940 for talks with Hitler and Ribbentrop. What Stalin wanted was a fresh "spheres of influence" agreement with Germany, removing German military presence from Finland and Bulgaria in the Soviet sphere, and a Soviet–Turkish understanding to secure Soviet control of the Black Sea Straits. Hitler refused this point-blank. He wanted Soviet participation in the Tripartite Pact, Soviet recognition of German hegemony in Europe and Soviet expansion southward. Acrimonious disagreement followed and the talks deadlocked when Molotov left on 14 November.

Left
Molotov with Reichsmarschall Hermann Goering (left). Goering had boasted that the Luftwaffe had destroyed the Royal Air Force. Sitting in an air raid shelter during the conference Molotov asked sardonically if Goering's claims were true, why was he (Molotov) sitting in an air raid shelter and what were those British bombers doing above him.

Above
Break for refreshments. Molotov seated far left; to the right, Ribbentrop is in conversation with Reichsführer SS Heinrich Himmler.

Left
Molotov's talks with Adolf Hitler and Ribbentrop began on the day he arrived in Berlin. It was Ribbentrop who had invited Molotov to Berlin. Stalin was cautious, the attitude assumed by Molotov in Berlin. Stalin wanted a new Nazi–Soviet Pact. Hitler and Ribbentrop rejected this outright and offered no concessions to Moscow.

"THE WINTER WAR" 1939–1940

The Soviet-Finnish war – the "Winter War" – was waged between 19 November 1939 and 13 March 1940, and did serious damage to the reputation of the Red Army due to its inept performance against "little Finland". Initial Finnish concessions failed to satisfy Moscow, and the Red Army launched its first, badly prepared offensive on 30 November. Nimble Finnish ski troops, prepared for winter war, harried the cumbersome, ill-trained Soviet troops. Red air-force attacks were largely ineffectual. On 12 February 1941, the Red Army unleashed a powerful offensive, heavy artillery smashing Finnish defences. Exhausted, the Finns sued for an armistice in March. The war cost the Red Army over 391,000 men, killed, missing or wounded.

Below
Red Air Force TB-3 heavy bomber, an obsolete machine, which suffered heavy losses in the war. The Red Air Force finally committed over 2000 aircraft to the "Winter War". Bombing raids on Finnish targets failed to disrupt troop movements or demoralize the Finnish population. Soviet losses were estimated at some 700 to 950 aircraft. The Finnish Air Force lost 70 aircraft.

Bottom
In February 1940, the Red Army began its second war with Finland. In forests like these, Finnish resistance cost the Red Army dear. On 11 February, massed Soviet artillery gave the Finnish defences a final battering. At the conclusion of the war Red Army casualties amounted to 391,783: 126,875 killed in action, missing, or died of wounds, and 264,908 medical casualties.

Above
A column of Soviet BA-32-3 armoured cars, armed with a 45-mm gun, on the move in Finland. Columns like these were easily ambushed by highly mobile Finnish troops trained in winter warfare. The Red Army deployed a minimum of 45 Rifle Divisions (5 Armies), and over 1500 tanks. It suffered severely from failing to win a speedy victory over the Finns.

RED ARMY REORGANIZATION

The fall of France in June 1940 severely agitated Stalin. It signalled to the Red Army to embark on a frantic policy of re-organization and re-armament. The mistaken decision taken in 1939 to disband the Red Army's large tank formations was hurriedly reversed. Stalin authorized the re-establishment of the mechanized corps. The war plan dating back to 1938 was urgently updated, mobilization plans revamped. Numerical expansion and technological modernization brought fresh turmoil, exacerbating existing problems. Officers and men had to be retrained, but time was running out. Worse, the new war plan was seriously flawed. Coupled with this was Stalin's "war avoidance" strategy, that left the Red Army in June 1941 unable either to attack or to defend.

Above
Marshal Semen Timoshenko, cigarette in hand, and General Georgii Zhukov on his left, inspecting field exercises in the Kiev Military District, autumn 1940. In May Timoshenko succeeded Marshal Kliment Voroshilov as Defence Commissar. Timoshenko introduced a new realistic training programme. Intensive training was backed up by iron discipline.

Left

Red Army "fast tanks" (BT-7-1) on exercises. On 22 June 1941 the Red Army tank-park amounted to 23,485 machines, of which 8000 were estimated to be for front line operations. In June, 73 per cent of older machines, BT tanks, T-28s, were undergoing repairs, 29 per cent major overhaul. Only a trickle of the new T-34 medium tanks and KV heavy tanks had reached the five frontier commands. By June, a mere 1475 had arrived (504 KVs, 967 T-34s).

Above

Instruction on a T-28B armed with a 45-mm gun. Produced between 1933–1940, the 3- turreted T-28, like many other Soviet tanks, was approaching obsolescence. The hastily re-formed tank and mechanized formations lacked both modern tanks and training. Driver-mechanics had only 1½–2 hours' experience of tank driving. Command staff for the most part lacked any real training in the handling of tank and motorized units.

1941

CATASTROPHE

Not until noon on Sunday 22 June 1941, was the population informed that the Soviet Union was at war, the war Stalin had manoeuvred to avoid or at least postpone. Even at this late stage he had struggled frantically to obtain clarification from Berlin and Tokyo. The "thunder from a clear sky" intensified by the hour. The wreckage of a thousand Soviet aircraft, shattered by Luftwaffe bombing, littered front-line airfields. Belatedly warned of an impending German attack, forbidden to implement full readiness, the Red Army was now ordered to contain enemy attacks before launching "a powerful counter-blow", a hopelessly unrealistic requirement in view of the havoc already wreaked by German guns and dive-bombers. Some regiments were fully manned, others needed several days to complete mobilization. German bombers targeted large cities near the front, destroying military administrative centres and cutting communications. Chaos ensued. The frontier commands were being torn to pieces, their situation changing by the hour from alarming to perilous.

The Soviet Union mobilized under fire. General mobilization succeeded in bringing some 5.3 million men to the colours. The Russian Orthodox Church responded ahead of the Communist Party. Patriarch Sergei of Moscow and All Russia called on all believers to defend Mother Russia, to defeat Fascism. Numbing shock began to wear off, but here was a highly militarized state without a functioning war machine. In Moscow, a preliminary wartime command system was hastily organized, although the High Command *Stavka* (General Headquarters) lacked a commander-in-chief. Administrative decree formally placed the Soviet Union on a war footing, the first of a flood of orders. One early decision, which formed the Industrial Evacuation Council (*Sovet po evakuatsii*) proved to be critically important and the first step toward a vast industrial migration that transferred men and machines into the eastern hinterland.

While Russia recoiled from the shock, the situation at the front rapidly deteriorated. Sixteen hours after launching Operation *Barbarossa*, the Wehrmacht had virtually unhinged the Soviet Northwestern and Western Fronts. The Western Front began to disintegrate. Government, Party and nation had yet to be fully energized. Stalin had failed to grasp the scale of military operations and the vastness of the war engulfing the Soviet Union. Only at the end of June, with Soviet divisions trapped in a giant German encirclement west of Minsk, did the terrible truth dawn. The Red Army was trapped in strategic maldeployment, its strength concentrated in the southwest while powerful Panzer groups attacked in the northwest and at the centre, closing on Leningrad and striking along the Moscow axis.

Stalin's nerve failed him at this point. Nevertheless, he recovered sufficiently to head a new, all-powerful body, the GKO (*Gosudarstvennyi komitet oborony*) or State Defence Committee, small in numbers but massive in authority. The high command was reorganized, a further step toward unifying the military and political direction of the war effort, culminating on 8 August with Stalin's virtual self-appointment as Supreme Commander of the Soviet Armed Forces (*Verkhovnyi glavnokomanduyushchyi*). He now held all key posts: chairman of the GKO, Defence Commissar and Supreme Commander. On 3 July 1941, Stalin finally broadcast to the nation, opening with unheard-of familiarity: "Comrades! Citizens! Brothers and sisters!" This would be a "people's war", patriotic, partisan, and unrelenting.

But Stalin's unprecedented personal appeal to his "brothers and sisters" was accompanied by the imposition of the savage "discipline of the revolver". Senior commanders were executed. The Western Front commander General Pavlov and his staff went before a firing squad. "Cowards and traitors" were summarily executed. Families were held accountable for soldiers taken prisoner or abandoning the battlefield. It was a system criminally profligate with soldiers' lives, one that brutally coerced or callously abandoned the civilian population.

The wreckage of the Western Front lay strewn over 200 miles (320 kilometres). The German haul of prisoners was staggering, reaching three million by December. Losses in weapons and equipment were on a stupefying scale: 20,000 tanks and 18,000 aircraft. Industrial evacuation gained momentum but, inevitably, industrial production dropped steeply in factories temporarily "on wheels".

The Wehrmacht drove ever deeper into Soviet territory, cutting off manpower and seizing resources. In the late autumn, the near-terminal crisis deepened. Leningrad was besieged, closed off to the outside world, suffering the first of 900 days of horror, hunger and cannibalism under German guns. Kiev fell on 18 September. Stalin's refusal to permit timely withdrawal trapped Soviet armies in another huge German encirclement. The Ukraine was all but lost. The German Army now marched on Moscow, triggering the "great panic of October".

Prime Minister Churchill had earlier promised, much to Stalin's relief, that Great Britain would not seek a separate peace with Germany. Now, in apparent desperation Stalin sought to do exactly that. He secretly sent out peace feelers to Berlin, proposing to cede the Baltic states, Bessarabia, even part of the Ukraine. The Soviet tactic was disguised by denouncing a supposed German offer of an armistice, a "peace offensive".

As in June, so in October, Berlin stayed silent. Germany was poised for complete victory in Russia. Another massive encirclement at Vyazma crippled Moscow's immediate defences. The Soviet government evacuated itself to Kuibyshev; Stalin wavered for 24 hours but decided to remain in the capital. The Moscow panic subsided and evacuation was organized more systematically: while 200 trains hurried civilians eastward, 80,000 railway trucks transported 498 dismantled factories out of the capital. Only 21,000 of Moscow's 75,000 metal-cutting lathes were left on site, and these were turned over to weapons production. Despite German bombing while factories were being shifted, one-and-a-half million railway wagons managed to shift two-and-a-half million troops to the front, and transferred 1,523 industrial plants to the east, 455 to the Urals, 210 to western Siberia, 250 to the Volga, 250 to Kazakhstan and Central Asia.

By late October, the industrial region of the Donbas had been overrun, Kharkov captured and the Crimea threatened. Moscow's outer defence line had been breached and German units were less than 50 miles (80 kilometres) from the Kremlin. In Berlin, the Chief of the Reich Press Office announced grandly that "Russia is finished". To many, Germans and Russians alike, the Red Army appeared to be on the verge of destruction while Soviet society lurched toward disintegration. All the signs pointed to society's vital signs failing, but complete disintegration did not follow. Enormous burdens had been heaped on the populace. Civilians were drafted to man the untrained, ill-armed militia, facing crack German divisions. Women, juveniles and the elderly had to compensate for failures to plan. Mobilization took men from the land, tractors were commandeered for the army, women harnessed themselves to ploughs, replacing the tractors and the draught animals.

The transition to "patriotic war" led to an intense campaign to identify the Communist Party with the Motherland, the abandonment of propaganda shibboleths coinciding with signs of a genuine, impassioned mood of national resistance. German atrocities, the manic killings, the brutal exploitation, the contempt for the *Untermensch*, massively encouraged resistance. The partisan movement was slowly gathering strength, while the Party used its "cadres administrations" to staff and direct partisan units.

Fortunately for the Soviets, complete collapse at the front and in the rear failed to materialize and Japan did not attack in the east. A two-front war would have doomed the Soviet Union. Soviet society showed an unexpected capacity to absorb immense damage and great ability to improvise amid chaos. Popular response was nevertheless uneven, dependent on local pride and local resources. The Communist

Party, acting as an administrative agent, operated indifferently, and, at the lowest levels, inflexibly. For a society long hardened to privation, the demands made upon it were frequently inhuman, but firm leadership produced results.

Much the same applied to the Soviet soldier. With proper leadership he fought tenaciously, only to be seized by sudden, inexplicable defeatism and panic that resulted in flight in the face of uncontrolled disorder. For all the years of repression and intimidation, basic moral resilience had survived in Soviet society, which was now fuelled by genuine patriotism and reaction to German barbarism.

The Wehrmacht failed to destroy the Red Army, terribly mangled though it was. As early as July, Stalin had ordered a ruthless reorganization into "small armies with five, maximum six, divisions", along with the abolition of corps administrations. Remnants of the lumbering mechanized corps were disbanded, and their few surviving tanks assigned to infantry support. A huge expansion in cavalry provided a temporary mobile force. Stripping artillery from divisions to form a High Command Artillery Reserve, employing direct fire and putting "the guns up front where they could see and hit the enemy" did much to save the Red Army. In November, Red Army strength dropped to its lowest ever: barely two million. But to the surprise and consternation of the German high command, fresh divisions and armies appeared in the Soviet order of battle: 18 fresh field armies had been raised from reserves and reductions in existing armies since July. Stalin very quickly grasped the importance of reserves, although the Red Army cried out for "trained forces in adequate strength".

Seas of autumnal mud, Russia's notorious *rasputitsa*, dragged the German drive on Moscow to a halt in late October. Clamped in seamless mud, both sides reinforced as best they could. On 6 November, anniversary of the Revolution, Stalin threw down a challenge in his speech: "If the Germans want a war of extermination, they shall have one". The *Blitzkrieg* had failed; the Red Army was still unbroken in the field. The next day, he reviewed a parade in Red Square of troops moving straight to the front line. Red Army front-line strength had recovered to almost 4,200,000 men supported by 7,400 aircraft and 4,490 tanks. To replace huge losses, 227 rifle divisions had been formed, 84 reformed and 143 rebuilt. In the north, Stalin ordered an attack to

prevent a fatal conjunction of German and Finnish forces and secure the vital "ice road" over Lake Ladoga, Leningrad's sole life-line. In the south, Timoshenko recaptured Rostov on 29 November. This German reverse, the first of any significance in the east, quickly ignited a crisis within the German high command.

Frosts hardened the ground. In mid-November, the Wehrmacht renewed its advance on Moscow. Improvised Soviet "composite groups" fought to hold off the pincers of a huge German encirclement. General Zhukov ordered a stand to the death. Red Army and German units grappled in freezing temperatures, both decimated and equally exhausted. Stalin dribbled reinforcements to the front, a handful of tanks here, packets of men there, all the while hoarding strategic reserves: 44 rifle and cavalry divisions and 13 brigades, sufficient for eight field armies. Zhukov scraped up his own meagre reserves.

On 4 December 1941, the final German thrust due east along the Minsk–Moscow highway was fought to a standstill in the city's outer suburbs. German units stood frozen in their tracks. German intelligence argued that Red Army reserves were exhausted: "no large reserve formations" existed. On 30 November, General Zhukov submitted his plans for a counter-stroke at Moscow. Stalin had secretly fed substantial reinforcement into three Fronts, Kalinin, Western and Southwestern, assembling a force of 1,100,000 men, 15 field armies, 774 tanks and 1,000 aircraft to power the Soviet attack. Timing was crucial. Stalin was convinced the German Army had dangerously overreached itself. Soviet and German strengths were now roughly equal. At 0300 hours on 5 December 1941, just two days before Japan's strike on Pearl Harbor, the Red Army attacked.

The tank divisions of the Western Front had pitifully few tanks, artillery was lacking and ammunition was available only to assault units. Zhukov relied on speed and surprise to compensate for large mobile forces, missing weapons and the lack of fully trained troops – his plan needed only a minimum of operational skill. For eight days the country heard little or nothing. Only on 13 December did Radio Moscow report Soviet successes to the north and south, announcing "the failure of the German plan to encircle and capture Moscow". Three days later, the Red Army turned to pursuit, harrying retreating German divisions.

ATTACK: SUNDAY, 22 JUNE 1941

In the early hours of Sunday morning, 22 June 1941, the German Army invaded the Soviet Union. In spite of being given repeated warnings of a German attack, Stalin had refused to order full military readiness on the frontiers. "The Germans must not be given any pretext for action against us", he reasoned. The Red Army was thus unable either to attack or defend.

Within hours, Soviet frontier guards were overwhelmed, the undermanned Soviet divisions caught in a maelstrom of fire, fast-moving German tanks and paralyzing bombing. Sixteen hours after the opening of Operation *Barbarossa*, the German Army had virtually unhinged two key Soviet Fronts, the Northwestern and the Western.

Above
At 0315 hours on 22 June, German guns opened fire.
Across the giant arc of the Soviet land frontier German troops
moved to their attack positions. With the mist and half light
to aid the attack, German infantry and armour slid out of their
concealment. Forward German elements, seen here, penetrated
Soviet positions and overwhelmed frontier guards, opening
passages for motorized and Panzer divisions ready to advance.

Left
German armour on the move at the beginning of a very long journey. Almost everywhere the Wehrmacht achieved tactical surprise. Soviet troops were caught in their camps and barracks and the Germans quickly overran incomplete or unmanned field fortifications.

Right
The front aflame. The pattern of heavy German bombing attacks, unexpected and punishing artillery fire "like thunder from a clear sky" and the assault on the Soviet frontier positions caused havoc among Red Army units. Russian units radioed plaintively, "we are being fired on. What shall we do?" They were reprimanded, but received no orders.

Above

0415 hours, 22 June. Advance units of the Seventeenth and Eighteenth Panzer Division, General Heinz Guderian's Panzer Group 2, begin crossing the River Bug. General Guderian had earlier observed that the strong points on the Soviet bank were unoccupied. At 0445 hours, leading tanks of the Eighteenth Panzer Division (seen here) forded the river. German "submersible tanks", equipped with waterproofing and able to move through 13 feet (4 metres) of water, had originally been developed for the invasion of Britain.

Above
These Soviet frontier troops had already been taken prisoner
before they realized that they were at war with Germany.
The first operational order issued to the Red Army mentioned
only "unprecedented aggression", not war. Frontier guards
fought back, and their wives, also in the firing line, fetched
water and ammunition and looked after the wounded.
Some of the women were also firing at the Germans.

Right

A captured Soviet soldier being searched by German soldiers. His chances of survival were slim. "After being interrogated who was the commander, the number of our unit etc., we were put behind barbed wire, kept without food or water. Then we were made to walk for three days (drinking water from potholes)." German troops organized the external guard. Among the prisoners the "politzei", volunteers from the prisoners, Tartars and Ukrainians kept order. Jews, Communists and Commissars, if discovered, were stripped to the waist, lined up and shot.

Left

German troops clear a village. Soviet civilians were ordered out of operational areas, most to make their way to what refuge they could find, others to be conscripted for forced labour and ultimate deportation. Animals were confiscated and houses frequently looted, then burned.

Opposite

German artillery observers spotting for targets. The initial German bombardment had put much of the Soviet artillery out of action. By noon, having flattened initial resistance and silenced Soviet guns, German Panzer and mobile forces in the northwest and at the centre were now set to strike out.

Above
Villages burned one by one along the route of the German
advance. As well as the villages, the crops burned.
Columns of dishevelled women and weeping children
left exposed villages, seeking what they supposed
would be safety in the towns. Others gathered in the
open fields, where German soldiers attempted to
convince them to return to what was left of their homes.

Left
Towns and cities, such as
this one, were also burned.
Here, two women take
refuge with a few, meagre
possessions in an improvised
shelter. Luftwaffe bombers
had rampaged over towns
and large cities in the frontier
military districts, destroying
the military administration,
buildings and communications
centres. Civilians were
caught up in both the heavy
bombing and the rapid
advance of German troops.

LOSSES

The Luftwaffe massacred the Red Air Force, destroying 1,811 aircraft in hours, of which 1,489 were on the ground. Huge losses mounted catastrophically: 20,500 tanks, thousands of aircraft and over three million prisoners of war by December 1941, most of whom were doomed to die. The civilian population suffered horrendously, callously left to their fate by the authorities or brutally coerced to dig trenches, take up rifles, or raise a local militia, and constantly threatened by the rapid German advance and harried by heavy bombing. Shortages were universal, made worse by falling production and appalling battlefield losses.

Above
German bombers – He111s, Ju 88s and Do17Zs – attack a Soviet airfield. "We hardly believed our eyes. Row after row of Soviet planes stood lined up as if on parade," said one Luftwaffe pilot. German aircraft carried out a devastating pre-emptive attack on 66 airfields in Soviet western military districts, where 70 per cent of Soviet air strength, mainly in the form of fighters, was deployed closed to the borders. The German air assault was concentrated against those airfields where the most modern Soviet aircraft were deployed.

Left
Wrecked Soviet aircraft.
On the first day of *Barbarossa*,
the Luftwaffe destroyed
1,811 Soviet aircraft for
the loss of only 35 German
aircraft, the greatest triumph
of aerial surprise attack in
aviation history. The heaviest
losses were at the centre of
the Soviet–German front,
where 520 aircraft were
destroyed on the ground
and 210 were shot down.
Aircraft in the Odessa military
district escaped this aerial blast
thanks to timely dispersal,
losing only three fighters.
Catastrophic though the
Soviet loss was, it could have
been even worse if all the
pilots had been casualties.

Below
Rivers – the San, the Bug, on
to the Dnieper – did not turn
out to be formidable barriers
to the German advance.

Above
Two dead Red Army soldiers, the
one behind the Maxim heavy
machine-gun still holding his
Mosin-Nagant rifle. Lightly armed
Soviet frontier guards were wiped
out almost to a man, frequently
fighting delaying actions with
suicidal bravery. In the absence
of air cover, Soviet regiments
moving up to the front line were
destroyed by German bombers.

Left
A dead Russian mortar crew.

Below
This message was carved
on a stone of the Brest
Litovsk fortress: "I am
dying. Farewell Motherland
but I am not surrendering.
20 July 1941." At 5 a.m.
on 22 June, fierce fighting
developed near the fortress.
Scratch units augmented
by units falling back on the
fortress took up the defence.
The fortress held out until 24
July, fighting from shattered
turrets and ruined emplace-
ments. Most defenders were
dead or wounded. In the
final phase, the few survivors,
among them the man who
carved the inscription on the
wall, mounted a last stand
in underground chambers
and tunnels, entombed
as they were in debris.

Left
Civilians help themselves to salt. All civilians suffered horrendously in the first weeks of the war. If they escaped with their lives, too much was heaped upon them. They suffered either from drastic and brutal emergency mobilization measures or mandatory orders. The very lowest echelons of the Communist Party proved to be inflexible. At the approach of the Germans, many Party members disposed of their Party cards.

Right
A Soviet woman and her children in the ruins of their home. Many of the villages in front-line zones had been heavily bombed and machine-gunned. Small villages and small towns had been virtually wiped out by German bombing, and their fields of rye and flax were left unharvested.

MOBILIZATION

The Red Army mobilized under fire, bringing more than five million men into the armed forces by the end of June. The Communist Party (CPSU) and Young Communist League – *Komsomol* – mobilized 95,000 men, of whom 58,000 were sent at once to the front as political instructors and agitators. Mass mobilization of the populace included the formation of "people's militia" (DNO) divisions, "home guard" units and compulsory participation in civil defence groups. Trade Union organizations and the Red Cross trained young women as front-line medics. Women and young girls volunteered for the front, the first of some 800,000 young girls and women to serve in the Red Army as nurses, pilots, snipers and tank crew members.

Above
War is declared and Moscow listens. Only at noon on Sunday 22 June did the Soviet government, through the mouth of Molotov, announce in a radio broadcast that the Soviet Union was now at war with Germany. The eight hours since the onset of the German attack had been spent partly in a final, frantic search by Stalin for a way to escape war. A flood of Soviet radio messages had been directed at the German Foreign Office, and even the Japanese had been asked for help.

Right
Anxious Muscovites listen as Molotov's radio broadcast continues: "The Government calls upon you, men and women citizens of the Soviet Union, to rally even more closely round the glorious Bolshevik Party, round the Soviet Government and our great leader Comrade Stalin. Our cause is just, the enemy will be smashed. Victory will be ours."

Left
Wartime mobilization proceeded relatively smoothly, initially bringing 5,300,000 men aged 23–36 to the colours. These were the first of a wartime turnover in manpower that amounted to 21,700,000. In all, 29 million men were mobilized. Processing the conscripts was the responsibility of the "military commissariats" at all levels. Men also reported to mobilization points or to units themselves.

Above

Off to the front. It is likely that new recruits would first be addressed by political officers. Few, if any, realized what awaited them. If they did suspect, then their confidence was more a product of propaganda than of rigorous training. Their early wartime letters reflected their mood and most carried brief assurances for the family, such as: "I am well. Don't worry". Others were more reflective, patriotic or touchingly valedictory.

Right
Instruction: elementary tactics, handling the rifle. By government decree on 29 June 1941, universal military training, or *Vsevobuch*, was introduced for all citizens between the ages of 16 and 65. New recruits to the Red Army who had not yet joined their units began training, along with local citizenry training for defence purposes, organizing special defensive measures and raising a militia (*opolchenie*).

Left
Red Army Recruits take the military oath: "I, a citizen of the USSR joining the ranks of the Red Army, take the oath and solemnly swear to be an honourable, brave, disciplined, vigilant fighter, strictly guarding military and state secrets ... I am always ready on the orders of the Workers-Peasants Government to defend my Motherland – the Union of Soviet Socialist Republics". The oath was read out to the recruits, who had to repeat it. Infringement brought swift retribution. Stalin's "Order No. 270" dated 16 August proscribed deserters, panic-mongerers and those who surrendered.

Above
Soviet recruit trainees bayonet fighting. Newly mobilized men were sent into units that were already disorganized, which only created more confusion, or they were thrown into "human wave" infantry attacks carried out with primitive or stereotypical tactics. They would march into machine-guns line abreast, advance in ranks 12 deep and ride in trucks side by side with tanks straight into German guns.

Right
Young woman learning to shoot using a Mosin-Nagant rifle with Model PE telescope. Young women and girls figured prominently among the early volunteers for the Red Army and for the front. Even without proper uniforms they headed for the front virtually in what they stood up, their plaits covered by head scarves. In August 1941, 10,000 "Young Communists", or *Komsomol*, many of them women, were sent immediately to the front to join the signals troops.

STALIN SPEAKS: 3 JULY

Molotov, not Stalin, announced a state of war on 22 June. Not until 3 July did Stalin speak publicly. Although the Soviet Union was at war, it lacked a war machine. The *Stavka* (High Command Headquarters) was hurriedly improvised. On 30 June, the all-powerful State Defence Committee (GKO) headed by Stalin was established. By August, Stalin held all the key wartime posts: Chairman of the GKO, Defence Commissar and Supreme Commander. Stalin's speech opened sensationally: "Comrades, citizens, brothers and sisters, fighting men of our Army and Navy. I am speaking to you, my friends." No apology for the Nazi–Soviet Pact was forthcoming from Stalin, only exhortation to intensive effort in the war. Little was said of the Party. This was "patriotic war", with help from the British and Americans.

Above
Soviet infantry seen marching past a slogan that reads, "Our cause is just, the enemy will be beaten, victory will be ours". These words, first uttered by Molotov on 22 June, became a massively emphasized theme in the "Patriotic War". At last, after days of unbroken public silence, Stalin spoke on 3 July, an extraordinary performance, which opened sensationally. Stalin had never spoken like this before. It was this that emphasized the gravity of the situation. The speech was one of "blood, sweat and tears" bearing comparison with Winston Churchill's post-Dunkirk speech.

Above
Recruits to the "Peoples' Militia", or *Opolchenie*, being
drilled, including a bearded veteran displaying his medals.
Poorly trained and badly armed "militia divisions", recruited
from the streets or from factory benches, were marched to
nearby front lines, notably, in the case of Moscow, Leningrad
and Odessa. Casualties were extremely heavy. The men
who survived subsequently formed regular Red Army divisions.

Above
German anti-Jewish propaganda poster: "The Jew is an
infection to the people". This was but one of countless
German propaganda posters designed to bolster their "crusade
against Jewish-Bolshevism" and to drive wedges between
groups in German-occupied territory. As the reality of German
rule – the atrocities, the killings, the deportations – became
more widely known, the posters became less and less credible.

Above
A 1941 poster directed to Soviet women:" JOIN THE RANKS
OF THE FRONT-LINE COMRADES, THE FIGHTING MAN'S
COMRADE, HELP-MATE AND FRIEND".This poster reflected
the tone of Stalin's 3 July speech, "Comrades, citizens,
brothers and sisters, fighters of our Army and Navy,"
one for all, all for one, the unity of front and rear,
stressing the contribution that women could and should
make — which, indeed, they did in magnificent style.

Above
A poster glorifying partisans: "GLORY TO HERO-PARTISANS, WRECKING THE FASCIST REAR". A graphic representation of Stalin's 3 July exhortation, "in the occupied territories partisan units must be formed…spreading the partisan war everywhere, for blowing up and destroying roads and bridges and telephone and telegraph wires."
The "intolerable conditions" which Stalin demanded the invaders should suffer took time to materialize. Not until 1942 did the partisan movement become widespread and effective.

Right
Stalin's son Jakov Djugashvili, prisoner of war (centre). Jakov, an engineer by profession, a senior lieutenant and battery commander of the 14th Howitzer Regiment, attached to the 14th Tank Division, was captured on 16 July 1941 near Vitebsk. On discovering that their prisoner was Stalin's son, the Germans attempted to exploit him for propaganda purposes, but did not succeed. Refusing privileges, he asked to remain with the rank-and-file soldiers. In all the photographs of Jakov, he deliberately refuses to look directly at the camera.

Не проливай свою кровь за Сталина!

Он уже убежал в Самару! Его собственный сын сдался в плен! Если сын Сталина спасся, ты также не должен жертвовать собой!

241 g

Left
A German leaflet directed at Red Army soldiers, inciting them to desert: "Do not shed your blood for Stalin! He has already fled to Samara! His own son has surrendered! If Stalin's son is saving his own skin, then you are not obliged to sacrifice yourself either!"

Left
Jakov Djugashvili, dead on the electrified wire of Sachenhausen concentration camp, 14 April 1943. Much controversy surrounds the fate of Stalin's son. Some believe it was suicide, others that the suicide story was a cover-up by the camp guards for a bungled attempt to prevent a suspected escape.
The German sentry Harfig shot him. After the battle of Stalingrad, Hitler suggested through the Swedish Red Cross that Jakov be exchanged for Field Marshal Paulus. Stalin refused, saying: "A marshal would not be exchanged for a lieutenant".

LENINGRAD BLOCKADED

On 8 September 1941, the German Army isolated Leningrad from the rest of Russia. Hitler decided not to storm the city but to reduce it by bombardment and starvation, the prelude to 900 days of unmitigated hardship, hunger and horror. There were 2,544,000 civilians in the city, 400,000 of them children and 340,000 in the suburbs, trapped in the greatest and longest siege endured by a modern city. The city held only peacetime food stocks. By November, people were dying of hunger – there was no food, no light, no heat and constant German shelling. More than a million finally perished from starvation, gunfire and disease.

Above
In this classic picture of the defence of Leningrad (now called St. Petersburg, its pre-Soviet name), anti-aircraft guns are being deployed in the neighbourhood of St. Isaac's cathedral. On 20 August, Marshal Voroshilov and Andrei Zhdanov, one of the key organizers of the city's defence, set up the Military Soviet for the Defence of Leningrad. Stalin objected because the Defence Soviet had been set up without his authorization and replaced Voroshilov with General Georgii Zhukov, who arrived in Leningrad on 10 September, announcing: "We are not giving up Leningrad. We are going to defend".

Right
"People's Volunteers" moving to the front. Men of the People's Militia (DNO) had been originally projected as the Leningrad Militia Army (LANO). The idea of forming 15 Militia Divisions was impossible without taking workers from the factories. On 4 July, it was decided to recruit three Militia Divisions in three days. Voroshilov decided to elevate worker battalions with the honorific designation "Guards".

Left
Take a tram-car to the front line! Tram-car No. 9 heading for the city limits. There, the conductor shouted: "Everybody off. This is the front. End of the line". People went to the front line passing through streets where they had gone to school as children.

Left
This famous picture shows victims of the German bombardment of Leningrad, the first of 65,000 citizens to die in the shell fire. On 4 September, German long-range siege guns opened fire on the city, shelling it day after day for more than two years. Shortly, the exchange of fire developed into a prolonged artillery duel between the counter-battery of Leningrad guns pitted against German siege weapons.

Right
The "Ladoga ice road". With the winter came ice and darkness. The ice on Lake Ladoga made a thin but solid connection between Leningrad and a Soviet shore-line. On 22 November, sixty lorries under Major Parchunov crossed the "Ladoga ice road", following the tracks of horses and sledges. This road become "the road of life", Leningrad's feasible but dangerous life-line, staving off disaster for a few more days.

49

ODESSA, SEVASTOPOL

"Odessa is not to be surrendered." Between early August and mid-October, the Red Army and Navy stubbornly defended the Soviet naval base. To reinforce the Crimea, Stalin agreed to the evacuation of Odessa, which was carried out with great skill. On 16 October, the last transport sailed for Sevastopol. In late

December 1941, Stalin planned to recover the Crimea, where Manstein's Eleventh Army was assaulting Sevastopol using fire from massive German guns. The Soviet amphibious landing on the Kerch peninsula in December temporarily relieved the pressure on Sevastopol, which held out until June 1942.

Above
Sergeant N.A. Lebedev's gun crew in action at Odessa. In 1941, the Black Sea naval bases, like other naval bases, lacked a scheme of land and air defence. The Black Sea Fleet and coastal defence secured the base against attack from the sea. The possibility of attack from the land or rear was barely considered. The fortification of Odessa began only on 12 July, when the threat from the land had become real.

Left
It was not Odessa but Sevastopol, whose ruins are shown here, that became the "Soviet Tobruk". The Germans had overrun the Crimea in October 1941 but had not subdued Sevastopol. Soviet plans envisaged the main threat coming from seaborne or airborne assault. The siege of the naval base began on 30 October. The first attempt in November, by General Erich von Manstein's Eleventh Army to take it off the march failed.

Below
The guns of the Black Sea Fleet played a vitally important role in beating back this first German assault on Sevastopol. The battleship *Paris Commune*, later renamed *Sevastopol*, is seen in action firing her main armament, 12-inch guns.

AID FOR RUSSIA

On 3 September, Stalin urgently sought Churchill's help, needing a "second front somewhere in the Balkans or France" and war supplies, raw materials and weapons. The Supply Conference met in Moscow at the end of September 1941, an important step in consolidating Anglo-Soviet wartime relations. Chaired by Molotov, the Beaverbrook-Harriman mission agreed to supply to the Soviet Union monthly stocks of weapons, tanks, guns and aircraft along with the raw materials copper, zinc and aluminium and 10,000 tons of armour plate. The first of the Arctic convoys carrying war material to Russia had sailed. British Hurricane fighters were also operating from airfields in northern Russia.

Above
British and American representatives: Lord Beaverbrook in the centre, William Averell Harriman on Beaverbrook's left, arrive in Moscow on 28 September for the Supply Conference. On the extreme left Andrei Vyshinskii, behind him Admiral Nikolai Kuznetsov, Commander of the Soviet Navy. Behind Beaverbrook is Sir Stafford Cripps, British Ambassador to Moscow.

Opposite, bottom
Loading tanks for Russia. The first of many convoys loaded with tanks and fighters set sail for Murmansk. At the Supply Conference, the Soviet representatives proposed the delivery of 1,100 tanks a month. It was decided that the British and Americans would supply 500, along with 300 light bombers, 100 of which would come from the USA. In addition, 1,000 tons of American armour plate would be delivered as an instalment on the Soviet order for 10,000 tons.

Right
The conclusion of the Moscow Supply Conference chaired by Molotov (front row 3rd from right). The Beaverbrook-Harriman mission evidently reached agreement on war supplies for the Soviet Union and monthly requirements of equipment. One very interested participant must have been Anastas Mikoyan (front row, third from left), a key figure in the Soviet wartime economy, head of Red Army supply and latterly involved in the Lend-Lease programme.

Left
Royal Air Force Hurricane fighters, 151 Wing, in Northern Russia. The Russians badly needed fighters to defend Murmansk. The first British convoy to North Russia included the veteran carrier HMS *Argus* carrying 24 Hurricanes. Fifteen more aircraft were crated and loaded on to a merchant ship. Once in range, the 24 aircraft on the *Argus* flew off to the Russian mainland, landing at Vaenga airfield, 17 miles from Murmansk. The crated aircraft were unloaded at Archangel and assembled, joining the Wing at Vaenga.

Right
A senior Soviet air commander tries out his newly arrived Hurricane fighter aircraft, which appears newly painted. The Red star on the port wing has been hurriedly over-painted on the Royal Air Force roundel, which is still just visible.

MOSCOW PREPARES TO FIGHT

On 6 October 1941, the German Army launched Operation *Typhoon*, which was designed to smash in the Moscow defensive concentration. One week later, the Moscow district staff ordered an emergency mobilization, with Zhukov commanding the Western Front. The State Defence Committee (GKO) mobilized the civilian population. A quarter of a million Muscovites, 75 per cent of them women, were drafted to dig trenches and anti-tank ditches. The "Moscow defence zone" was established, dividing Moscow into three sectors to the front and three lines to the rear. Factories were prepared for demolition and bridges were mined. Many fled but a resolute minority remained, Stalin included.

Right
On 12 October, *Pravda* warned the citizens of Moscow of the "terrible danger" threatening the capital. All citizens were to mobilize, prepare for the coming battle and organize defences both on the approaches to the city and within the city. These women are digging anti-tank ditches along the highways into Moscow, part of three massive defence zones.

Left
Women welders at the Hammer and Sickle factory producing anti-tank "hedgehogs", which obstructed the tanks' progress. The workers in Moscow's concrete and metallurgical factories were ordered to produce more "hedgehogs", barbed wire and reinforced concrete for gun positions. Women workers at a lemonade bottling factory prepared "Molotov cocktails" to be used against tanks. Factories making household goods now produced mines.

Right
Sandbags protecting shop windows in Moscow against air attack. German bombing raids continued, although not on the same scale as in July. By night, Moscow reverberated with the sound of anti-aircraft guns deployed on roof tops and in open squares.

Above

A famous wartime picture: crowds gather at the underground station on Revolution Square in Moscow, where a shot-down Ju-88 bomber has been put on display with several of its defused bombs.

Left

An anti-aircraft gun deployed on a Moscow roof top, the Kremlin in the background. The ferocity of Moscow's anti-aircraft defences surprised the Luftwaffe. Other fronts were starved for air cover and air defence, but in Moscow, General Mikhail Gromadin, commander Moscow Air Defence Zone, had I Anti-Aircraft Corps with 796 guns and VI Air Defence Fighter Corps with 600 fighters, including the 2nd Independent Night Fighter Squadron.

Above
The ubiquitous Moscow barrage balloon is seen here deployed on Tver Boulevard near the Bolshoi Theatre. In addition to fighters, anti-aircraft guns and barrage balloons, the defence of Moscow involved a huge programme of camouflaging the city. Mock factories were built, the walls of the Kremlin were painted over to resemble house-fronts, Lenin's Mausoleum was sandbagged and roads were painted to resemble rooftops.

Right
The Mayakovskii underground station. The Russians had been expecting the blitz on Moscow and underground stations were used for emergency accommodation, mainly for the elderly and mothers with young children. All stations provided first-aid posts and rudimentary enclosed latrines and some even had small libraries. Bunks or camp beds were supplied for women, children and the elderly. Smoking was forbidden!

Left
Muscovites from the Kiev district of the city build more barricades, but many fled from Moscow. The "great panic" occurred on 16 October – there was a rush for the railway stations and the roads east of Moscow were jammed with lorries and cars moving east. Many offices and factories stopped working.

Right
Actors from the Moscow Theatre donating their valuables for the state defence fund. Like many other Muscovites, the actors responded to patriotic appeals and the sense of danger. Workers and actors from the Bolshoi Theatre had already appeared in the Lenino District of Moscow digging anti-tank ditches. After the "great panic", Moscow recovered its nerve. Moscow Radio announced that Stalin was in the city and would remain there, which had a positive effect on morale.

INDUSTRY MOVES EAST

In 1941, the Soviet Union embarked not only on the greatest industrial migration in history but also on a second industrial revolution. The Evacuation Soviet began work in early July to shift major armaments plants to the east. At first, improvised evacuation worked badly: dismantling took place under air attack and railway lines were bombed. But between August and October, a staggering 80 per cent of Soviet industry was "on wheels". The railways accomplished a stupendous task, using one-and-a-half million trucks to transfer 1,523 factories eastward. Moving the factories was one problem, starting up production was yet another. Machinery began operating even as new factory walls were erected around it.

Above
In his broadcast of 3 July 1941 Stalin issued immediate "scorched earth" instructions: "The enemy must not be left a single engine…not a pound of bread or a pint of oil. Collective farmers must drive away all their livestock, hand their grain reserves to the state authorities for evacuation to the rear." In scenes like these, collective farmers with their pigs and cows carried out Stalin's instructions, all to the rear.

Above
A classic scene of industrial evacuation that must have been replicated
many thousands of times. Plans were drawn up in July to establish a
"second line of industrial defence" in the eastern hinterland. Whole
factories were transplanted, not only from those industries threatened by the
German advance. The manufacture of armour plate was transferred
eastwards, the manufacture of tank engines was immediately transferred
from Kharkov to Chelyabinsk in the Urals. Evacuation also facilitated the
conversion of industries to war production. With the machines and
equipment went the workers and the technical staff, often whole families.

"PARTISAN WAR"

On 18 July 1941, the Central Committee issued instructions for the conduct of "partisan war" and the Party apparatus, the *Komsomol*, the NKVD and the Red Army were all involved in organizing the movement. The initial results were meagre and scattered, but the long arm of Soviet authority was at least re-emerging. The population was increasingly squeezed between German and Soviet-partisan pressures, but anti-German feeling was growing and the idea of a "patriotic war" was intensifying. Senseless, self-defeating and brutal German occupation policies, mass-murder rampages and vicious anti-partisan actions steadily alienated the population. The first public hanging of a partisan had already taken place.

Left
Soviet partisans in 1941 taking the oath to "work a terrible merciless revenge upon the enemy". The partisan and his family swore to die rather than surrender. Stalin overcame his deep suspicion of irregular warfare, and his speech of 3 July called for the organization of partisan units. Partisans like these, young and old, men and women, were not in the beginning a serious fighting force because they lacked arms and supplies.

Below
Partisans laying demolition charges. In the early stages of partisan warfare, the mission of partisan units in the immediate and deep German rear was to slow the German advance, where possible sabotaging the German communication network. Soviet partisans also attacked German supply dumps, sabotaged equipment and hid farming equipment in the forests.

Above
A meal for Red Army soldiers in the enemy rear. Many Red Army soldiers and Party officials had been marooned behind German lines and soldiers from retreating units escaped into woods. Here, a Red Army unit is receiving help from the local population. Eventually, NKVD officers and Party and Komsomol members were infiltrated through German lines to organize and support partisan units.

Above
The hanging of Soviet partisans in the Moscow region.
The German authorities reacted savagely from the outset
to partisan warfare, or *Bandenkreig*. Partisans and their
supporters, or suspected supporters, were liable to instant
death. The most brutal reprisals were authorized at the
highest level, even by Hitler himself. The German hostage
order stipulated that 50–100 hostages should be shot
for every dead German soldier. This was the opening
scene in an expanding war of terror and murder.

Right
The first public execution in German-occupied Russia was the hanging of Masha Bruskina on 26 October 1941. Masha was the precursor of thousands who were rounded up and publicly hanged with placards round their necks, intended to be an example to the rest of the population.

Left
Partisans on the move in the forests and swamps that typically formed partisan hideouts. Partisans faced an appalling existence, living in constant fear of betrayal to the Germans, who could buy informants for a handful of marks. Spies and traitors were executed by partisans as a matter of course. In some areas, partisans were given food and shelter, in others they were betrayed or killed. The population came off worst when trapped between two sets of reprisals, the German and Soviet authorities.

Opposite
A standard execution. When partisans blew up the Continental Hotel in Kiev, Headquarters of the German Sixth Army, all Jews were ordered to report for "resettlement". They were marched to the outskirts of the city, taken in small groups, lined up against the pit some 18 feet (5 metres) long and eight feet (2.5 metres) deep and shot.

Right
Execution: a shot in the back of the head, carried out with a certain grim intensity, even relish. Nazi indoctrination was widely held accountable for the younger officers' obeying of criminal orders, while there was a general feeling that German soldiers were culturally superior. German officers felt a contempt for the *Untermensch*, the "sub-human" Slav, coupled with a disposition towards anti-Semitism and militant anti-Bolshevism. German officers and men were constantly reminded that this was "a war of ideological extermination".

Left
The bodies of civilian victims, taken hostage and shot by the Germans, left lying in a schoolyard at Rostov-on-Don.

Overleaf
The mass execution of Soviet prisoners of war and civilians by a German firing squad from an unidentified unit.

67

Left
Such was the scale of the German slaughter in Russia that the German command was hard-pressed to find the most efficient form of extermination, particularly with respect to the Jews. Some German commanders disliked the inhumanity of hanging. The preferred method of the *Einsatzgruppen*, the SS extermination squads, was to round up all Jews and shoot them out of hand. Here, a "standard" execution is watched by a youth (centre), a member of the Nazi youth labour organization.

Right
Public hangings such as these became more frequent, even routine. Bodies were left hanging in public places as a deterrent to members of the resistance, partisans and those displaying "anti-German" sentiments or committing "anti-German" acts. A man was hanged, suspected of having punctured German tyres. He was hanged along with another, unknown, man. Both were left hanging for three days in full view. No one was allowed to cut the bodies down.

Left
German soldiers hang Zoya Kosmodemyanskaya, a member of the *Komsomol*, a volunteer for active service, who was sent behind German lines as part of a sabotage unit. She was taken prisoner while attempting to blow up a German ammunition dump. She was stripped and tortured to the extent that even some German soldiers were sickened. Covered in blood and half dead, she was taken to the gallows with a placard around her neck denouncing her as a partisan. Zoya posthumously became a decorated Hero of the Soviet Union and an inspiration for poems and films.

Right
A grieving Russian mother. As the extent and reality of the German atrocities became widely known throughout Russia, the will to resist stiffened and the "patriotic war" became in reality a "people's war", but the cost to soldier and civilian alike was horrendous, as this mother attests.

"A WAR OF EXTERMINATION"

"If the Germans want a war of extermination, they shall have one," said Stalin in his speech of 6 November 1941, which was delivered while German armies were less than 50 miles (80 kilometres) from Moscow. The next day, Stalin held the traditional military parade in Red Square. Riflemen, old T-26 tanks, and a few new, formidable T-34 tanks crossed Red Square, moving straight off to the nearby front line. Aware of the risks, Stalin had summoned General Zhukov to discuss the parade and enquire about German intentions. German troops were regrouping, Stalin was told, and no major attack was imminent. Moscow's air defences were strengthened against a possible air attack but neither ground assault nor air-raid materialized.

Above
The reviewing stand at the Kremlin, 7 November 1941.
From left to right: Molotov, Marshal Budenny, Stalin, Georgii Malenkov, Mikoyan and Aleksandr Shcherbakov. Marshal Budenny is obviously prompting Stalin. The previous day, Stalin had delivered his speech on the anniversary of the October Revolution, the "war of extermination" speech. On 7 November Stalin spoke out even more brutally, dismissing fears that "the Germans could not be beaten", mocking it as the panic-talk of a bunch of frightened intellectuals, reminding his listeners that in 1918 the Red Army had been in a worse position.

Right

The Red Square parade on 7 November was traditional. Stalin wanted the parade but he was not prepared to take risks and questioned Zhukov about the likelihood of a German attack. Zhukov replied that nomajor attack was expected in the next few days, though air defences must be reinforced and fighter aircraft must be moved up to form new Fronts. Stalin's speech meant to steady Russia's nerve. This sombre Moscow parade had a dramatic impact and was regarded as a brave, even defiant act.

Below

Red Army motorcycle units, their side-cars equipped with DP light machine-guns, form up for the 7 November parade in Red Square. The parade was of great military importance, most of the units involved moving directly to front-line positions, but was also a political act of great symbolic significance.

Right
Women and men working to finish anti-tank defences on Bolshaya Kaluzhskaya Street in Moscow. It looked as if these defences were going to be needed: on 15–16 November, the Germans resumed the attack on Moscow.

Left
The famous welded anti-tank "hedgehogs" blocking a Moscow thoroughfare. During 1941, the face of Moscow changed. Anti-tank obstacles were set up in most streets, many more anti-aircraft batteries were deployed and barrage balloons were concentrated. When not working in the factories, teenagers were engaged in fire-watching.

Above
Women workers in a Moscow factory producing mortar bombs
under the slogan: "Our energy, our strength, our life – all
for the defence of Moscow!" Moscow factories underwent
rapid conversion to military use. The Kalinin and SAM
factories produced Katyusha rocket launchers and
machine-guns, the Moscow car factory produced
Shpagin machine-guns, while the Red Proletariat
machine-tool factory turned out mines, shells and fuses.

Left
Fourteen-year-old Sasha tends his machine in a Moscow arms factory. A great deal of untrained labour, including youngsters like Sasha, their numbers supplemented by many who had been driven out of the villages in the area of Moscow, housewives and grandmothers now worked in factories.

Below
Women workers take time off for machine-gun instruction. The atmosphere in Moscow was now visibly military, prepared for any eventuality, and the "Moscow panic" of October had long since subsided.

THE MOSCOW COUNTER-STROKE: 5 DECEMBER 1941

On 15 November 1941, the German Army opened its "final offensive" against Moscow. Ten days later, German units closed on Moscow to the north, just 20 miles (32 kilometres) from the Kremlin. As temperatures plunged, decimated German and Soviet units grappled with each other in the very suburbs of Moscow.

The Red Army struck first on the flanks, Tikhvin in the north, Rostov in the south. Meanwhile, Stalin carefully husbanded his reserves. On 5 December 1941, the Red Army launched its Moscow counter-blow. Eight days later, the Soviet press broke its silence to announce the repulse of the Germans at the gates of Moscow.

Left
On the left, Marshal Timoshenko seated at a Hughes teleprinter machine. Behind him, Nikita Khrushchev, member of the Military Soviet of the Southern Front. On 9 November, Timoshenko had submitted a plan to Stalin to attack the flank and rear of First Panzer Army in the south. The *Stavka* had ruled out any reinforcements, forcing Timoshenko to regroup before he could launch his attack.

Left
Timoshenko and Khrushchev studying the battle map with Lieutenant Colonel Ivan Bagramyan, Chief of Operations. Soviet and German divisions at Rostov moved simultaneously in attack and counterattack on 17 November. German tanks had penetrated the northern suburbs of Rostov. The Soviet objective was now the liberation of Rostov and a drive on Taganrog. On 29 November, Soviet divisions cleared Rostov and the Wehrmacht suffered its first major reverse, with far-reaching consequences for the German command.

Above
From the streets of Moscow straight to the front line, which was dangerously near. On the morning of 28 November, German units were circling Moscow to the north and were no more than 20 miles (32 kilometres) from the Kremlin.

Above
Major General Konstantin Rokossovskii, commander of the
16th Red Army at Istra stands second from right, with Divisional
Commissar A. A. Lobachev and Colonel Afanasii Beloborodov,
commander of the Siberian 78th Rifle Divison. Also present was
the writer Vladimir Stavskii, who was subsequently killed in
action aged 43. Istra was a key point in the defences along the
Volokolamsk Highway. Beloborodov's Siberians were deployed
along the Istra river and at the high dam of the Istra reservoir.

Above
Planning the Moscow counter-stroke at Western Front HQ.
From left to right: Lieutenant General Nikolai Bulganin,
Member of the Military Soviet, one of Stalin's "super-
commissars"; Western Front commander General Zhukov;
Chief of Staff Colonel General Vasilii Sokolovskii; and
General Ivan Khokhlov, (Supply), member of the Military
Soviet. On 30 November, Zhukov had presented
his plans to Stalin and the *Stavka*. The objective
was the destruction of the two German armoured
wedges that lay north and south of Moscow.

Above
Destroyed German equipment at Klin. The Red Army's counter-
stroke opened on 5 December 1941. In the battle for Moscow,
both the Red Army and the German army had fought almost
down to their last battalions, but Stalin had skilfully husbanded
reserves. In the battle of the "Klin bulge", Zhukov's troops
attempted to destroy Panzer Groups 3 and 4. By noon on
7 December, forward Soviet units were over-running the
Headquarters of LVI Panzer Corps outside Klin. Klin had
assumed enormous significance as the lynch-pin of Panzer
Group 3 and the hinge of Army Group Centre's left wing.

Left
Red Army attacks developed
across more than 500 miles
(800 kilometres), stretching
from the north to the south
of Moscow. Zhukov gave
orders to avoid frontal
attacks wherever possible.
Soviet tactics depended
on mobile pursuit units like
those in the photograph,
their function being to cut
German lines of retreat and
create maximum confusion.

Right
A Soviet infantry patrol with
dogs, man and dog alike
in snow camouflage.
Dogs were trained to carry
explosives and ambush tanks.

Above
Soviet troops launched their offensive as temperatures dropped steeply and with snow lying three feet (a metre) thick. German troops suffered severely from the shortage of winter clothing, but at least Soviet infantry (pictured here) was adequately dressed. However, the ferocious weather did hamper Soviet operations: the Red Army suffered from a desperate shortage of motor lorries, resulting in insufficient supplies of food and ammunition, so horse-drawn sleighs had to be substituted for lorries.

Left
General Zhukov lacked the large tank formations that were needed for the planned breakthrough: the six tank and motorized divisions of the Western Front had virtually no armour. In the absence of large mobile forces, Zhukov turned to the cavalry, notably Major General Pavel Belov's 1st Guards Cavalry Corps and Major General Lev Dovator's 2nd Guards Cavalry Corps. Casualties were inevitably heavy in breakthrough operations or raids into the German rear and General Dovator was killed in action on 20 December 1941.

Above

A battery of Katyusha multiple-rocket launchers, nicknamed "Stalin's organ", in operation. In 1940, the Main Artillery Administration had placed orders for experimental M-13 rockets, but in the same year a 16-rocket launcher was developed and mass production was authorized on 21 June 1941. The Red Army first used the Katyushas on 14 July 1941 and the results were reported as "excellent". The Katyushas were a formidable bombardment weapon much feared by the Germans and were closely guarded, usually hooded in canvas, manned by elite units designated "Guards Mortar Regiments".

Above
A deserted German sentry box on the outskirts of
Moscow. By mid-December, the results of the Red
Army counter-offensive had become vastly encouraging:
the German Army had been driven away from Moscow,
removing the immediate threat to the city, and the Red
Army had made great progress on the northern and southern
flanks. But the German centre had as yet to be unhinged
and the Panzer groups had so far escaped Zhukov's traps.

Left
In Volokolamsk, west of Moscow, a boy removes German road signs following the town's liberation in late December 1941. Zhukov was not convinced that the "Lama-Ruza line" was the limit of the German withdrawal and had on 20 December issued fresh orders for an advance beyond this line.

Right
A German cemetery in Russia. For propaganda reasons, Stalin had grossly exaggerated German losses. Nevertheless, the Wehrmacht had suffered very severely. The total number of Germans killed by mid-December 1941 amounted to 775,078 men. During the second German offensive against Moscow, from 16 November to 5 December, the Soviet authorities' calculations of German losses were: 55,000 killed in action, 100,000 wounded or severely frost-bitten and 777 tanks lost.

1942

RECOVERY

At the end of the first week of January 1942, the Red Army went over to a general offensive across the entire Soviet–German front. The success of the Soviet counter-offensive at Moscow, officially terminated on 7 January, persuaded Stalin that "the Germans are in disarray, they are badly fitted-out for the winter". The moment had come to attempt the destruction of German forces near Leningrad, west of Moscow and in the south. German Army Group Centre, still a threat to Moscow, was the prime target. The Leningrad Front received orders to relieve Leningrad, now in desperate straits, and destroy Army Group North. In the south, the Red Army was to attack Army Group South, liberate the industrial region of the Donbas and free the Crimea.

The Soviet General Staff had already drafted these offensive plans in mid-December 1941. The destruction of all three German Army Groups was to be a prelude to "driving them westward without pause", exhausting their reserves. In the spring, the Red Army would have powerful reserves, the Germans few. The eventual prospect of "the complete destruction of the Hitlerite forces in 1942" mesmerized Stalin. On 5 January 1942, he presented his grandiose "war-winning" plans for the further conduct of the war to an enlarged session of the *Stavka*. General Zhukov protested. The entire plan was a distortion of reality. Rather than concentrating on the destruction of Army Group Centre and exploiting the success of the Western Front, Stalin proposed to expand outward with every Soviet Front. Chief economic planner Voznesenskii supported Zhukov. The necessary supplies to support simultaneous offensives on all fronts were simply not to hand. Stalin disagreed: "We must grind the Germans down with all speed, so that they cannot attack in the spring." General Zhukov had argued in vain. Attack directives had already gone to Front commanders before the *Stavka* meeting. Stalin issued categorical orders: offensive operations must continue without delay, without waiting for the final assembly of assault formations.

By the end of February Stalin's attempt to seize the strategic initiative had failed. Soviet uninterrupted offensives were dashed against the rocks of German resistance that implemented Hitler's "Stand Fast" order. Leningrad remained blockaded. At the centre, for all its deep and dangerous thrusts, Zhukov's offensive was flagging. Parachute troops were no substitute for men, mobility and firepower. In the south, Timoshenko hacked his way into Army Group South but failed to achieve a major breakthrough. Late in March, Stalin's first strategic offensive shuddered to a halt.

Stalin now considered the summer campaign. Ostensibly agreeing to move to "the provisional strategic defensive", he secretly gave orders for "partially offensive operations", including a huge, three-front operation in the south planned for May. Stalin had some grounds for optimism. The Wehrmacht had lost a third of its strength. Red Army order of battle reportedly amounted to 400 divisions supported by 10,000 tanks and 11,000 aircraft. The economy was reorganized to sustain protracted war. Enduring great hardship, Soviet workers increased output, producing 4,468 tanks and 3,301 aircraft between January and March 1942. Tank corps reappeared and tank armies formed up. The Red Army was slowly emerging as a more viable fighting machine. But "to attack and defend simultaneously" invited disaster.

In early April, Hitler's attention was fixed on the flanks, concentrating "main operations in the southern sector", destroying the Red Army west of the Don, driving toward the Caucasus oil fields. Stalin concluded that Moscow and the "central region" would be the German target. Evidence to the contrary he dismissed as "disinformation". He planned to hold advanced positions at the centre, de-blockade Leningrad and liberate Kharkov and the Crimea. German intelligence predicted the "Kharkov offensive". British intelligence advised Moscow that the Germans were forewarned and preparing to strike. Timoshenko attacked on 12 May 1942, north and south of Kharkov. Five days later the German counter-attack developed. Timoshenko's armies ran straight into a trap, into encirclement and disastrous defeat, but Stalin and the *Stavka* refused to call off the offensive. Appalling clusters of Russian dead were piled high on the edges of German gun-pits. Only 27,000 men escaped alive from the encirclement and Red Army losses amounted to more than 250,000 men. The entire Soviet southwestern axis lay in ruins. Stalin erupted in a fury. For the first time he used the word "catastrophe".

Worse was swiftly to come. Incompetence bordering on criminality led to further huge losses in operations aimed at clearing the Crimea, blunders that forced Soviet troops off the Kerch peninsula, a "ghastly mess" costing 176,000 men. German guns moved to reduce the fortress of Sevastopol, a fiery prelude to Manstein's final assault with Eleventh Army. Far to the north, General A. A. Vlasov's 2nd Shock Army, fighting to free starving Leningrad from the agonies of unbelievably nightmarish siege conditions, had been trapped for some time. Deprived of rescue, 2nd Shock finally succumbed in June. General Vlasov was taken prisoner and elected to join the Germans, bent on raising his "anti-Stalin liberation army".

To plug these huge rents torn in the Red Army, Stalin, convinced that Japan was wholly committed in the Pacific, drew on his Far Eastern armies to replenish his reserves. Adamant that Hitler was aimed at Moscow and cunningly encouraged by a German deception operation (Operation *Kremlin*), Stalin continued to pile armour and reserves on the Western and Bryansk Fronts. The reality was Hitler's Operation

Blau (Blue), which aimed at the final destruction of the Red Army. Two huge German pincers striking from the north and south were to meet west of Stalingrad between the Don and the Donets, where they would squeeze the life out of remaining Soviet resistance, followed by a drive into the Caucasus. Dismissing intelligence reports, Stalin persisted in believing this to be a German "feint", berating his intelligence officers for not having uncovered the real German intentions.

Germany had regained the strategic initiative in the east. Anticipating "further great trials", Stalin set out on a search for a Second Front, despatching Molotov to London and Washington in late May 1942. The signing of the Anglo–Soviet Treaty was a step forward, but it did not produce a binding commitment to opening a Second Front. Nevertheless, Stalin believed it did, which was the cause of resentment and recrimination when Churchill met Stalin in Moscow in mid-August.

At the end of June, "great trials" undoubtedly beset the Soviet Union, inducing a sense of disaster and precipitating a huge crisis. The Wehrmacht unleashed Operation *Blau* on 28 June 1942, unmistakably driving southeast, finally forcing Stalin to begin redeploying divisions held in reserve at Moscow, which were desperately needed by Soviet armies in the south. Marshal Timoshenko's Southwestern Front, already badly weakened by the May defeat, was torn apart by General Paulus's Sixth Army. The threat to Timoshenko's rear now spread to Malinovskii's Southern Front, which was battered by the German Seventeenth Army and First Panzer Army.

The *Stavka* wound up the Southwestern Front on 12 July 1942 and replaced it with the Stalingrad Front commanded by Timoshenko, stiffened with three reserve armies, armies that had yet to detrain and deploy. Available infantry undertook gruelling forced marches to a front line largely unknown to their commanders. Stalin now accepted the inevitability of withdrawal in the southeast. The General Staff wanted no more "stand fast" orders, no repetition of the disasters of Kiev and Vyazma. The Red Army would hold Voronezh to contain German forces otherwise moving southward. Timoshenko and Malinovskii received timely orders to withdraw. Holding German forces at Voronezh gave Timoshenko time to pull his battered divisions over the Oskol, the Donets and the Don, an orderly withdrawal covered by rear-guard actions fought in classic Russian style. The Red Army escaped to the east and south.

By redeploying his reserves, Stalin aimed to maintain pressure at the centre and on the northern flank. At the end of July, the Western and Kalinin Fronts attacked the bulging Rzhev salient. In the Leningrad area the Red Army, reinforced with additional armour and artillery, renewed its offensive operations. The aim was tie down German reserves. In the south, the Soviet command struggled to organize its defence. Hitler divided Army Group South into two separate elements: Army Groups A and B. Three days later, on 13 July, he abandoned the idea of a rapid advance on Stalingrad. The German Sixth Army under Paulus would advance on Stalingrad alone; 40 Panzer Corps was detached to Rostov, where Hitler planned a giant encirclement battle that would deliver the coup de grace to a Red Army already "finished".

After 50 hours of ferocious fighting, Rostov fell on 23–24 July 1942. Soviet authorized, organized withdrawal robbed Hitler of a super-encirclement he hoped would surpass anything seen in 1941. Stalin, however, deliberately misrepresented this as "unauthorized withdrawal", personally editing the draconian *Order No. 227* dated 28 July, indicting the Red Army for having failed the country. "Not a step back" literally meant what it said: no space was left for further retreat. The penalty for cowardice and retreat was the bullet, the result wanton, indiscriminate shooting. Stalin ordered Stalingrad, the city bearing his name, on to a war footing, turning an industrial city into a fortress and mobilizing the local population. A dangerous situation became perilous. Soviet defences in the Don bend had been breached and the Fourth Panzer Army was moving up from the Caucasus. Stalingrad was now doubly threatened, from the northwest and the southeast.

In early August, Army Group A had broken into the Kuban and was racing for the northern Caucasus. The massed refugees and overpowering precision of the German *Blitzkrieg* echoed scenes from 1941. On 15 August, the German Sixth Army went over to the offensive northwest of Stalingrad, Paulus's divisions making hazardous assault crossings of the river Don. One week later, on 23 August, a massive Luftwaffe onslaught on Stalingrad killed thousands and inflicted terrible damage. German tanks followed, racing across 35 miles (56 kilometres) of open steppe to break into Stalingrad's

northern suburb and reach the Volga. Stalin was incandescent with rage, convinced that Stalingrad would be lost within days. German tanks and infantry attacked from all sides, but contrary to German expectations, Stalingrad did not fall. One of the most terrible battles in the history of warfare had only just begun.

Hitler persisted in regarding the Russians "as all but finished". German intelligence was more realistic. Soviet reserves did exist. Soviet factories were producing more modern tanks, T-34s and KVs. German armies were increasingly dispersed, their flanks exposed, while Red armies were concentrating. Amid the appalling carnage inside Stalingrad, where each building was fought for, Zhukov and Vasilevskii outlined a counter-offensive plan. The situation of German troops on the "Stalingrad axis" looked increasingly unfavourable. The Soviet plan outlined two "operational tasks": encirclement and isolation, followed by the annihilation of the main German force in Stalingrad. Meanwhile, inside Stalingrad the bridgeheads must be held at all costs.

On 13 October, Stalin signed the "decision map" for Operation *Uranus*, the Stalingrad counter-offensive. But the real secret was that the Red Army planned *two* major, mutually supporting counter-offensives, Operation *Mars* at the centre and Operation *Uranus* in the south, timed for 19 November and 24–25 November respectively.

Hitler terminated the German offensive on 14 October, planning the "final destruction" of the Red Army in the coming winter campaign. Inside Stalingrad, Soviet defenders were at their last gasp, Chuikov's 62nd Army failing fast. The *Stavka* gambled that the final German attack would fail, that Paulus could not move to the defensive and that his deployments remained unchanged. Early in November, Soviet divisions moved to their start lines. On the eve of *Uranus,* Soviet forces on the Stalingrad axis numbered over a million men, 894 tanks and 1,115 aircraft. Chuikov was instructed to stand by for orders. At 0730 hours on the misty morning of 19 November 1942, Soviet guns opened fire. While *Uranus* succeeded brilliantly, *Mars* fared disastrously and was finally abandoned on 20 December, having cost the Red Army half a million men. After 100 hours of offensive operations at Stalingrad, the Soviet outer encirclement was complete. At the end of November, more than 20 German divisions and elements of two Rumanian divisions, totalling 300,000 men, had been trapped. The agony of Paulus's Sixth Army had only just begun.

STALIN'S FIRST STRATEGIC OFFENSIVE

In January 1942, Stalin launched the first Soviet strategic offensive of the war, now intent on nothing less than the destruction of all three German Army Groups, North, Centre and South. On 7 January, convinced that the Germans were on the point of collapse, Stalin ordered attacks across the entire Soviet–German front. Army Group Centre's forces encircling Moscow were a priority target. Offensive operations were also directed to relieve blockaded Leningrad and liberate Orel, Kharkov and the Crimea. For all its remarkable performance, the Red Army lacked sufficient firepower and mobility to destroy Army Group Centre. Elsewhere, Soviet offensives finally ran into the ground, the result of Stalin's over-optimism.

Right
In the first week of January 1942, the Red Army went over to the general offensive. These troops of the 4th Parachute Corps were used by Zhukov to assist in the Vyazma encirclement operation. He launched operations in mid-January and mid-February to break the German front from the rear.

Left
A firewood sale takes place in Moscow, January 1942. Moscow was still under a state of siege, and the city's central heating system was not working. People were hungry: food reserves had dwindled, bread rations remained at about 1½ lbs (750g) per day and vegetables were very scarce.

Above
"Let's give our Soviet soldiers warm clothing and boots." This was one of the many Soviet campaigns that not only supported front-line soldiers, but also assisted orphaned children and helped rehabilitate wounded soldiers.

Right
A frequent sight early in the morning in Moscow: young women marching on their way to military exercises. Moscow's air defences had been substantially reinforced and young women such as these were assigned to anti-aircraft batteries and the observer corps.

Below
There were few children left in Moscow. Those who remained were regarded with special affection as they played. As Ilya Ehrenburg said: "Perhaps it was because everybody wanted a glimpse of the future". Here, grandmothers keep watch as children play near barrage balloons.

LENINGRAD'S "ROAD OF LIFE": 1942

A huge and terrible famine had begun in Leningrad, where the first blockade-induced deaths from starvation occurred in December 1941. Lack of fuel brought transport and factories to a halt. Bread rations had already been cut five times and people resorted to eating cottonseed oil cake. Winter brought ice to Lake Ladoga, temporarily connecting Leningrad with the Soviet shore. In late November, the first lorries had crossed the precarious Ladoga Ice Road, the city's "Road of Life", staving off immediate disaster. By February 1942, several roads had been built over the ice, but Leningrad's high death rate persisted until April 1942.

Left
The "Ladoga Ice Road" was Leningrad's precarious life-line during the ghastly winter of 1941–42. The first lorry made the dangerous trip on 20 November 1941. Only 800 tons of flour had been moved by the end of the month, but this staved off complete disaster. The "Road of Life" worked, despite continual bombing by German aircraft.

Right
Evacuees at Lake Ladoga. Many evacuees flowed into and out of Leningrad, and some 55,000 refugees were brought into the city during the 1941–42 winter. Orders were given on 6 December to use the "Ice Road" to evacuate 5,000 people per day. By 22 January 1942, an estimated 36,000 individuals had been evacuated by this route. In all, almost a million people were evacuated.

Above
Did this little Leningrad girl survive? At the start of the
Ladoga Ice Road, the "Road of Life", a monument in the
form of a huge stone flower was erected to the children
of Leningrad who died in the blockade. Children were
evacuated from the city in June and early July 1941, but
had moved into the path of the German advance and
were returned to Leningrad. Some, but not all, were
evacuated eastwards for safety. Every effort was made
to keep the calorie content of the food given children
left in the city to 684 calories, most of it from bread and
a little meat and fat.

Left
Children suffered cruelly. The diary of Tanya Savicheva, an 11-year-old Leningrad schoolgirl, recorded the deaths of her family one by one. Many children were orphaned and were looked after in children's homes.

Right
Traffic was a rare sight during Leningrad's winter. Children's sledges appeared, conveying the feeble, the dying and the dead. This street scene shows a bulletin board, which listed articles for sale and barter and family news. The bulletin board was a prominent feature of the Leningrad blockade.

Left
General Kirill Meretskov decorates a very young Red Army soldier. Meretskov, who commanded the Volkov Front, launched a premature attack south of Leningrad in January 1942. His troops were dispersed, untrained and badly supplied. This failed attempt to lift the Leningrad blockade was followed by the subsequent tragedy of Vlasov's 2nd Shock Army.

Overleaf
Leningrad had survived the terrible winter of 1941–42. With the spring came the big clean-up. Meagre rations were supplemented by vegetables grown on any available plot like this one in front of the Isaakievsky Sobor (St. Isaac's Cathedral). But the high death rate due to the blockade persisted.

"ALL FOR THE FRONT": THE WAR EFFORT

In 1942, the Soviet war industry had begun to recover from the massive chaos inflicted on it by German occupation and losses due to relocation. The Soviet economy now geared up for protracted war. Industrial managers, workers, pensioners and juveniles all worked furiously to increase output. Heavy-tank production was transferred to the Urals, while Moscow and

Kuibyshev turned out ground-attack aircraft. At the price of great hardship and personal sacrifice, Soviet workers increased output, producing 4,861 tanks and 3,301 aircraft between January and March. Each quarter that year showed successive increases, culminating in a grand total for 1942 of 21,681 combat aircraft and 24,446 tanks.

Right
People used their savings to buy a tank or an artillery piece. Communities and collectives, such as this Moscow kolkhoz, banded together to fund a tank column consisting of T-34s. In 1943, the Russian Orthodox Church supplied funds for a tank column named "Dmitrii Donskoi".

Below
In 1942, Stalin said, "The IL-2 is as vital to our Red Army as air or bread." The IL-2 shturmovik was a highly successful ground-attack aircraft. Its production centred on Kuibyshev and Moscow. The two-seat IL-2 was flight-tested in 1942 and mass-produced in 1943.

Above
In Moscow, as elsewhere, workers were offered extra pay and food to increase production. Teenagers, housewives and grandmothers worked in the munitions factories. Women were also sent to the wrecked mines of the Moscow coal basin to dig coal, drive locomotives and operate mining machines.

Right
During mass- production of the deadly IL-2 shturmovik, the slogan was "All for the front, all for the victory". These aircraft appear to be two-seat shturmoviks, the rear machine gun eliminating the vulnerability of the earlier single seat IL-2. A total of 36,163 IL-2 shturmoviks were sent to the front.

Left
A worker reads a letter sent from the front to munition factory workers. Red Army soldiers made frequent visits to war factories, and factory workers paid visits to front-line units to see the results of their labour. These workers are well wrapped up and range widely in age.

Above
This T-34 tank, under construction in a tank factory in Irkutsk, carries the name of Zoya Kosmodemyanskaya, an 18-year-old Komsomol activist and partisan who was tortured and executed in 1941. The T-34 medium tank became the mainstay of the Red Army. It was modernized in 1943, emerging as the T-34/85.

DISASTER IN THE SOUTH: SPRING–SUMMER 1942

In the spring and early summer, the entire Soviet southern wing collapsed under the weight of German attacks. Hitler had determined on Operation *Blau*, driving south to the oil of the Caucasus and on to Stalingrad. Timoshenko's May offensive to recover Kharkov ended disastrously with catastrophic losses: 240,000 men and 1,200 tanks. At Kerch in May, Mekhlis squandered 21 divisions of three Soviet armies in a nightmare of confusion and incompetence, losing 176,000 men and almost 350 tanks. The Soviet defeat at Kerch now greatly facilitated Manstein's final assault on fortress Sevastopol in June.

Right
On the left, Lieutenant General Nikita Khrushchev; on the right, Colonol Leonid Brezhnev, political officer. Brezhnev had himself inserted in Zhukov's memoirs through a wholly fictitious incident, to enhance both his image and stature during the Great Patriotic War.

Left
On the morning of 12 May 1942, Marshal Timoshenko (centre), commanding the southwestern theatre, launched the disastrous Kharkov offensive. Five days later, German offensive operations had cut into Timoshenko's rear. The *Stavka* ordered the Kharkov drive to continue, but Soviet armies were being encircled: 200,000 Soviet soldiers were taken prisoner.

Above
One of the victims of the
"ghastly mess", the disaster at
Kerch in May 1942, is killed
in action. The German assault
completely overwhelmed
the Crimean Front command.
The incompetence of Lev
Mekhlis cost the Soviet
Crimean Front 176,000
men, most of its 350 tanks
and about 3,500 guns.

Right
This Soviet navy *razvedchik*,
or scout, belonged to the
Black Sea Fleet, which
played a major defensive
role during the siege of
Sevastopol. At dawn on
7 June 1942, General
von Manstein's Eleventh Army
opened the final assault on
fortress Sevastopol, which
had held out for 250 days.

Left
Major General Ivan Petrov, commander of the Coastal Army from October 1941 to July 1942, at an observation point. General Petrov had already played a significant role in the defence of Odessa in October 1941, supervising a very successful evacuation. On 29 June, Petrov discussed evacuation orders for the Sevastopol garrison.

Right
Sevastopol had held out for 250 days, a siege during which the Black Sea Fleet played a major defensive role. Soviet navy sailor squads and marines made up 20,000 of the 106,000 defenders, and showed themselves to be staunch, determined defenders who performed many heroic acts. Soviet guns were silenced only by direct German hits.

"NOT A STEP BACK!": STALIN'S ORDER 227

On 28 July, four days after the fall of Rostov, Stalin issued his Draconian Order No. 227: "Not a step back!" Defeat had followed defeat and Russia was in great danger – Hitler was convinced the Red Army was all but finished. The Soviet southern Fronts had collapsed, and the Red Army now fell back behind the Don, where it managed to escape encirclement. German Army Group A was now able to strike into the Caucasus. While German armies advanced into the Great Bend of the Don, three Soviet armies were rushed in to reinforce the newly established Stalingrad Front. But Hitler had already abandoned plans for a rapid attack on Stalingrad – Paulus's Sixth German Army would plunge on to Stalingrad alone.

Right
The Red Army defends Voronezh during Operation *Blau*. Stalin believed that the fresh German offensive was a prelude to an advance on Moscow and that German armies would swing north once they reached Voronezh. Voronezh was fiercely defended by the Red Army and its fall finally persuaded Stalin that the German offensive was moving southwards.

Right
On 12 July, Timoshenko's Southwestern Front was practically ripped to pieces. Hitler was determined to fight another great encirclement battle at Rostov. After the fall of Rostov on 23 July and the capture of the great bridge over the Don, Stalin issued the savage order No. 227: "Not a step back".

Above
The huge encirclement at Rostov eluded Hitler as the Red Army pulled out of danger. Covered by rear guards, Timoshenko's troops had begun a withdrawal toward and over the Don. The withdrawal was on a large scale and it was orderly, demonstrating the traditional Russian mastery in rear-guard fighting. A woman medic tends a wounded soldier in the foreground.

Left
Orderly withdrawal continued, but at a cost. This Red Army soldier was shot while crossing a stream.

Above
Soviet infantry General Malinovskii's Southern Front. An infantry section to the left is deploying to attack, covered by the soldier with the Degtyarev DP drum-fed light machine-gun. This very successful weapon was used throughout the war. The rifleman holds a Mosin-Nagant Model 1891 7.62mm bolt-action rifle with fixed bayonet.

Above
Soviet infantry Southern Front.
Riflemen hold their Mosin-Nagant
rifles, the standard infantry weapon.
The machine-gunner in the
foreground is firing the Maxim Model
1918 heavy machine-gun equipped
with a shield, here without its Sokolov
wheeled mounting.

"A SECOND FRONT": WHERE, WHEN?

The Anglo-Soviet Treaty was signed in London on 26 May 1942 during Molotov's visit to London. In July, the Soviet position in the south became critical. Soviet demands for a Second Front and a renewal of suspended British convoys intensified. On 12 August, Churchill met Stalin in Moscow. Stalin put up a bitter fight for a Second Front, accusing the British of being afraid to fight, and joint staff talks achieved little. However, news of the proposed Anglo-American landing in North Africa cheered Stalin somewhat. The atmosphere evidently improved, and the final Churchill-Stalin meeting on 15 August was "more cordial".

Right
Soviet Foreign Minister Vyacheslav Molotov (seen here fourth from the left in a helmet and flying suit), lands in Scotland after a flight in a Russian TB-7, a four-engine heavy bomber. On 20 May, he travelled from Dundee to London by train, stopping discreetly at a small station short of the capital to be met by the Foreign Secretary.

Left
The signing of the Anglo-Soviet Treaty in London, on 26 May 1942. From left to right: Soviet Ambassador Ivan Maiskii, Soviet Foreign Minister Molotov, Foreign Secretary Anthony Eden, and Prime Minister Winston Churchill. The Treaty established an alliance between the United Kingdom and the Soviet Union that would remain valid for 20 years.

Above
Eight convoys sailed for Russia
in 1941, 13 more in 1942, all
of them subject to heavy air
and submarine attacks.
HM Submarine P614,
shown here in Arctic waters,
sailed with Convoy QP14
heading west. P614 sighted
U408, stalked the U-boat and
fired torpedoes, which missed.

FROM "PARTISAN WAR" TO "PEOPLE'S WAR"

Throughout 1941, political work among partisans and in the occupied territory intensified, with the aim of transforming random partisan activity into a mass-movement "people's war". The extent of German occupation (45 per cent of the population, 47 per cent of agricultural land) inevitably expanded the scale of partisan activity. The creation on 30 May 1942 of the Central Staff of the Partisan Movement marked a key step in establishing Party and state control of partisan formations and the local populace. The Central Partisan Staff, under Panteleimon Ponomarenko, maintained communications with the partisans, co-ordinated their activities, organized co-operation with the Red Army and supplied training and weapons.

Above
Soviet partisans drive Germans from a blazing village. Stalin summoned experts on partisan warfare to talks at the Kremlin in August 1942 – men like Sidor Kovpak, commander of partisan forces deep in the German rear. Discussions covered equipment, weapons, links with the occupied population and the role of commissar.

Right
In 1942, "partisan regions" were set up, often in areas where there were no Germans and where partisans had re-introduced Soviet authority. This photograph is set in the famous "partisan region" of Porkhov, in Leningrad province.

Above
A mounted Soviet partisan detachment in Northern Osetiya. Red Army troops and partisans successfully defended Vladikavkaz, the region's capital, after the Germans were forced by blizzards to abandon an attempt to break through to the Black Sea across high mountain passes.

Right
Soviet partisans and their families were subject to the most savage reprisals by German regular troops and pro-German auxiliaries. The deportation or shooting of villagers accused of "partisan sympathies" were widespread activities. The civilian population suffered twice over, as partisans would root out suspected collaborators. This man typifies the suffering and despair.

Below
"The Red Army soldier must fight to the last drop of blood." Stalin's *Order No. 227* meted out severe punishment for "panic-mongers, cowards and traitors". These Soviet troops are shooting a deserter out of hand. In the battle for Stalingrad, a reported 13,500 men were executed. During the entire war, the Red Army recorded 376,300 deserters.

Right
The partisan retribution was swift and deadly. Civilians who collaborated with the Germans or who took up local government posts under the Germans were singled out for elimination. Punishment was especially savage in partisan units, where suspected traitors were hunted down and killed.

Left
This appears to be a specially posed propaganda picture. The figure on the right, well-dressed, well-fed, armed and relaxed, was one of the former Soviet prisoners who were recruited from prisoners to provide rear security or support for German units; they were known as the *Hiwis (Hilfswillige)*. Others were recruited to fight with the Ostlegionen.

Above

With men at the front, women and juveniles took over work on the land. Tractors had been mobilized to tow guns for the Red Army, and women pulled ploughs in place of draught animals. They lived up to their banner, "All for the front, all for victory over the enemy".

THE WEHRMACHT ON THE VOLGA

At dawn on 23 August 1942, units of 16th Panzer Division, Sixth Army raced across 35 miles (56 kilometres) of steppe, and by nightfall had reached the Volga at Spartanovka, a northern suburb of Stalingrad. That same day, one of the most terrible battles in modern times had opened when Richthofen's bombers launched a devastating attack on Stalingrad, causing heavy loss of life. Stalin received the news of the German breakthrough with curses and anger. Workers were mobilized to reinforce the Red Army. Every plant and factory was turned into a miniature fortress amidst hurried preparations to fight inside the city itself.

Right
This scene from Stalingrad is reminiscent of the chaos of 1941. German troops closing on Stalingrad in 1942 forcibly cleared the civilian population from German operational areas. The columns of those deported extended for many miles, and few provisions were made for them.

Left
In 1942, Stalingrad was being turned inside out. The evacuation, which had been halted earlier, was now resumed. Factory equipment, stores, livestock and people were shipped in increasing quantities over the Volga. The city itself and the surrounding steppe were dotted with groups of men and women moving up to the bank of the Volga. Inside Stalingrad, the streets were blocked with improvised barricades.

Left
Two key commanders at Stalingrad were Colonel General Andrei Eremenko, left, and Nikita Khrushchev, right. Stalin first appointed Eremenko Commander of the Southeastern Front, but in a command reshuffle he took over the Stalingrad Front. Eremenko arrived there on 4 August 1942. He was met by Nikita Khrushchev of the Military Soviet of the Stalingrad Front.

Right
On 23 August, General Wolfram von Richtoffen's Fliegerkorps VIII launched a massed bombing raid on Stalingrad, destroying the administrative and residential centres and inflicting huge casualties. On the Volga, the docks burned to their shell. Oil storage tanks were set ablaze, spreading a dense pall of smoke.

Left
German tanks reached the
Volga on 23 August 1942.
Heavy German bombing
had destroyed factories
and machine shops, but
amid the ruins, workers were
repairing weapons.
At the last minute, still clad
in overalls and work clothes
like the men pictured here,
the people of Stalingrad
picked up rifles and
ammunition to join
Red Army soldiers.

Left
By mid-September, Stalingrad had become a mass of destruction and annihilation along the bank of the Volga. Entire divisions had vanished: 8,000 men were reduced to about 200, armed with rifles and a few machine-guns. The population continued to build anti-tank defences, fitting out buildings for defence by riflemen like those shown here.

Right
Close-quarter combat in Stalingrad was unbelievably deadly and ferocious. Paulus pleaded for reinforcements to help in the house-to-house fighting, which was killing off his infantry. Small Red Army "storm groups", typified by these few men street-fighting from shattered buildings, were ideal for lightning attacks, counter-attacks and ambushes.

Right
The most stupendous surge of fighting that Stalingrad had seen so far developed on Monday, 14 October. Five German divisions, three infantry and two Panzer, 300 tanks and air support moved in a "major assault" designed to overrun the factory districts. The battle for the Tractor Plant over, German troops are seen here inspecting what was left of the factory. An entire Soviet division, 37th Guards, had been wiped out defending it. Fighting for the "Red October" factory was only now building up, but promised to be no less savage.

Left
A solitary Red Army signaller makes his way through ruins. During the hours of daylight in Stalingrad movement was kept to a minimum, so much lay bared to German observation and to German bombers overhead. Only at night did city "traffic" start up, criss-crossing the slit trenches linking strong points, fortified basements, supply points for food and water, and other basements housing company and battalion headquarters.

"GROUND SOAKED IN BLOOD": STALINGRAD OCTOBER–NOVEMBER

General Chuikov's 62nd Army fought to the bitter end for every factory, street and house in Stalingrad. Divisions and regiment were broken down into heavily armed, small "storm groups", ideal for lightning attacks and counter-attacks. Volga ferries under heavy fire shipped men and ammunition into the city, but the loss of the central landing stage posed great dangers for

Chuikov, cutting off his support. Stalin repeatedly demanded that "Stalingrad must not be taken by the enemy". In mid-October, the 62nd Army, split in two and consisting of 47,000 men and only 19 tanks, survived a terrible firestorm. In November, "at their last gasp" and fighting for every last metre, the defenders were promised "the kind of help you have never dreamed of".

Right

Lieutenant General Vasilii Chuikov, the 62nd Army commander and defender of Stalingrad, is seen here in his headquarters, the "Tsaritsa bunker", second from left. Over-exposed to German fire, Chuikov was permitted to change location but was nearly burned alive when the oil-storage tanks above his new HQ were bombed.

Left

In northern Stalingrad, the massive concrete blocks of three huge factories, the Tractor Plant, "Barrikady" and "Red October", formed natural forts together with blocks of workers' apartments. Red Army soldiers and workers defended the factories tenaciously, fighting for every shop floor and machine. General Chuikov estimated that no fewer than five German Divisions fought to take the Tractor Plant. Here German soldiers inspect the ruined factory.

Left

Unbelievably, incredibly, thousands of civilians, such as these, lived out their lives amidst the maelstrom of the Stalingrad fighting. They found refuge in holes in the ground, in cellars or ruined buildings, in sewers, even shell-holes within the ruins of a city under relentless bombardment. Finding not only food but also water became a nightmare. Men and women scavenged, seeking what they could amidst dead men and dead horses. Under cover of darkness, children ventured out to search for scraps. Countless civilians not killed by German bullets or blown to bits succumbed to infections and poisons.

Below

General Vasilii Chuikov, commander of the 62nd Army defending every inch of Stalingrad, stated that "city fighting is a special kind of fighting. The buildings in a city act like breakwaters." These "breakwaters" dispersed advancing enemy formations, making German forces go along the streets. After each battle the Stalingrad "breakwaters", resembled this scene, mounds of rubble sprouting solitary half-shattered walls, often with floors still attached but hanging in empty air, Soviet infantry cautiously clambering about.

Right
A burned-out arms factory and discarded bombs that will never reach their targets. The Luftwaffe rained its own bombs ceaselessly on major Soviet factories. On the afternoon of 29 September, more than 100 German aircraft bombed Stalingrad's Tractor Plant, destroying the outbuildings and setting the workshops alight.

Left
Came November, came the snow. The defensive operation in Stalingrad was drawing to a close. Chuikov's 62nd Army had been squeezed into a tiny bridgehead but still held fast. The defensive battle for Stalingrad from July to November cost the Red Army 643,842 men killed, missing or wounded.

TRANSFORMATION AT STALINGRAD: OPERATION URANUS

Wbile ferocious, inhuman fighting raged inside Stalingrad, the idea of a Stalingrad counter-offensive – Operation *Uranus* – gained ground after mid-September. The counter-offensive would involve two stages, the first aimed at encircling German troops at Stalingrad, establishing a solid outer encirclement to isolate those forces, the second designed to destroy encircled German divisions and defeat attempts to break into the Soviet "ring". On the eve of *Uranus*, Soviet forces numbered over one million men armed with 894 tanks. Soviet artillery opened fire on 19 November 1942. After 100 hours, five Soviet armies had encircled the Paulus's Sixth Army inside Stalingrad, trapping 20 German divisions.

Left
In November 1942, the Red Army launched two strategic operations: *Mars*, the brainchild of Zhukov, which aimed to envelop Rzhev and smash Army Group Centre; and *Uranus*, the planned encirclement of the German "Stalingrad Group". *Mars* employed the Kalinin Front, commanded by General Maksim Purkaev, and the Western Front, commanded by Colonel General Ivan Konev, pictured here. *Uranus* was launched on 19 November and succeeded brilliantly. *Mars* began on 25 November and was a disaster, costing 335,000 casualties and 1,600 tanks.

Below
General Konstantin Rokossovskii (left), Don Front commander, observes the course of operations. In the murk of Thursday morning, 19 November, the Soviet Southwestern and Don Fronts launched the Stalingrad counter-offensive, joined a day later by the Stalingrad Front. In little more than 100 hours, on 23 November Soviet units linked up at Sovetskoe, south-east of Kalach, completing the outer encirclement. On 30 November the inner encirclement close, trapping 22 German divisions, including Sixth Army.

Left
Red Army troops fighting in the Rzhev salient. Konev's Western Front and Purkaev's Kalinin Front were to encircle the German "Rzhev Grouping", capture Rzhev and free the Moscow–Velikii Luki rail link. Both Germans and Russians suffered heavy losses in ferocious fighting. Zhukov defied reality, continuing to attack while Soviet losses in men and tanks mounted disastrously. By 15 December, *Mars* had failed. Stalin and the *Stavka* knew this; even Zhukov knew it. Rzhev did not finally fall until 3 March 1943.

1943

THE TURNING POINT

The unbelievable, the unthinkable, occurred at Stalingrad on 31 January 1943. The German Sixth Army surrendered. Newly promoted Field Marshal Friedrich von Paulus, 24 German generals and 2,400 officers became Soviet prisoners of war. Military operations ceased at 1600 hours on 2 February. It remained only to round up prisoners and bury the dead. Germany was in mourning, the Soviet Union jubilant, its survival finally assured. The Red Army reaped its reward: gold braid, decorations and formal rank insignia befitting a professional army and promotions to Marshal, an elite into which Stalin shortly elevated himself. With the tinsel came the steel: five new tank armies assembled in January 1943, powerful shock forces urgently needed by the Red Army.

Stalin again prepared multi-Front offensives along three strategic axes: the southwestern, western and northwestern. The *Stavka* aimed to entrap 75 German divisions and liberate the Ukraine, and also to encircle Army Group Centre and break into Army Group North. Stalin pursued twin objectives: the destruction of German forces in the field and the recovery of territory. Even before the German surrender at Stalingrad, Operation *Iskra* had pierced the blockade of Leningrad on 18 January, re-establishing a direct overland link with the rest of Russia and slowly alleviating terrible hunger and inhuman privation.

Early in February, a gigantic duel in the south had opened – the prize was Kharkov, second city of the Ukraine. Red Army forces closed upon it at some speed, recapturing it on 16 February and tearing a 100-mile (160-kilometre) gap between two German Army Groups. The Soviet armies fanned out, aiming for the Dnieper crossings, which,

once secured, would trap the entire German southern wing. German tank columns were moving but not, as Soviet intelligence mistakenly believed, to cover a withdrawal. Field Marshal Manstein attacked, blocked the Soviet advance to the Dnieper, restored the situation between the Dnieper and the Donets and struck toward Kharkov. By 10 March, German units were fighting inside Kharkov's suburbs.

The spring thaw and the mud halted both the Soviet winter offensive and the German counter-stroke. The Red Army put German losses at over one million men between November 1942 and March 1943, almost 100 German and "satellite" divisions destroyed. The entire Soviet–German front was visibly foreshortened, its most striking feature the huge Soviet "Kursk salient" jutting westward. It presented the Red Army with positions from which to strike the flanks of German Groups Centre and South, hence Hitler's preference for a rapid attack after the thaw. Stalin and the *Stavka* clearly understood the danger as crack Panzer divisions began assembling on both sides of the salient.

After March, the longest lull of the war set in. Both sides prepared for a decisive encounter: the battle of Kursk. The key Soviet decision was to let the Germans lead off. Though sorely tempted, newly elevated Marshal Stalin was effectively dissuaded from attacking first. Fortification of the salient was reorganized and developed systematically, massive defences sited in great depth. Artillery poured into the salient, part of a huge investment into firepower and mobility for the "new" Red Army. Soviet designers worked furiously to meet the challenge presented by the latest German Mark VI Tiger and Mark V Panther tanks. Hitler procrastinated, in spite of Manstein's warning that delay invited disaster. Not until mid-June did he fix 5 July as the date for Operation *Zitadelle* (Citadel), the offensive at Kursk a demonstration of German superiority, the road to final victory, the victory "to shine like a beacon round the world".

The battle of Kursk was one of the greatest armoured jousts ever seen. Fifty German divisions, including 19 Panzer and motorized divisions, 3,155 tanks, supported by 2,600 aircraft, were committed to eliminating the Kursk salient in a double envelopment. The German Ninth Army deployed on the northern face of the salient, the Fourth Panzer Army and "Army Detachment *Kempf*" on the southern face in the Belgorod area. Two Soviet Fronts, Central and Voronezh, deployed 1,272,700 men, 3,275 tanks and 25,000 guns and mortars. To block any final German breakthrough, the *Stavka* assembled its largest-ever strategic reserve at General Konev's Steppe Front, no fewer than 449,100 men and 1,506 tanks and assault guns.

The German offensive opened in the early hours of 5 July 1943. In the north, Rokossovskii checked the German Ninth Army, launching immediate counter-attacks using his new 2nd Tank Army and reserves. Within a week, the Ninth Army was completely halted and started to withdraw on 14 July. On the southern face, the German commanders used Tiger tanks to break into the third Soviet defensive belt to a depth of some 20 miles (32 kilometres), only to be stopped by the 1st Tank Army. Short of a complete breakthrough, German forces in both the north and south were unable to effect encirclement, but on 11 and 12 July, the Fourth Panzer Army penetrated the 1st Tank Army's defences, precipitating the massive tank battle at Prokhorovka. The Soviet command decided upon a general counter-attack using five armies, two from Steppe Front reserves. Over 1,000 tanks were engaged in the battle for Prokhorovka: the 5th Guards Tank Army reinforced with two additional tank corps charged over open ground, literally ramming German Tigers and Panthers, losing 400 tanks out of 800 in this furious engagement, destroying in turn 320 German tanks.

As a major offensive operation, *Zitadelle* had been smashed beyond recovery. Manstein pleaded for more time to finish off Soviet armoured reserves, but Hitler had already called off the offensive, withdrawing Panzer units to deal with the Anglo-American landing in Sicily. Losses in individual Panzer divisions verged on the calamitous and

infantry divisions were torn to tatters. General Guderian called the failure "a decisive defeat". After Prokhorovka, Soviet tank strength was halved – losses in anti-tank guns were particularly heavy, battle casualties standing at 177,847. Twelve months after the Stalingrad counter-offensive was unleashed, the situation had taken a profound turn in favour of the Soviet Union. The killing ground at Kursk confirmed German premonitions of disaster born of Stalingrad, miles of fire consuming Panzer divisions and burning out infantry. The last victories of the German Army in Russia had come and gone.

The rapidity of the Soviet breakout after the blood-letting at Kursk took the German command by surprise. In the north, three Fronts eliminated the "Orel salient", the 3rd Guards Tank Army taking Orel itself on 5 August. To the south, Manstein thought Soviet forces too weakened to attack, but after a brief pause, an enormous Soviet attack unrolled along the Belgorod–Kharkov axis. Belgorod was heavily defended, Kharkov the key to the German defence of the eastern Ukraine. Konev's Steppe Front stormed Belgorod on 5 August, leaving him free to fight the fourth and final battle for Kharkov. The city Hitler was determined to hold at all costs was officially liberated at noon on 23 August.

Stalin speedily escalated the scale and scope of the Red Army's summer–autumn offensive, seeking decisive success in the Ukraine and Belorussia. The destruction of German forces in the southern wing was to be effected in the Donbas and the eastern Ukraine. The North Caucasus Front was to eliminate the German Seventeenth Army in the Kuban. Stalin intended to hurl Soviet armies to the Dnieper on a broad front, pre-empting Hitler's plan to fortify the *Ostwall* – the defensive rampart designed to secure the western Ukraine and Belorussia. In spite of the battering Soviet armies had taken since early July, the Soviet command managed to assemble 2,633,300 men, 2,400 tanks, 2,850 aircraft and 51,200 guns and mortars on this southwestern axis. Partisan forces were also assigned a specific role in the *Stavka's* plans: 20 partisan groups comprising 17,000 men operating in the western Ukraine were committed to sabotaging German lines of communication, intensifying the *relsovaya voina*, the "war on the railway tracks".

Though the *Ostwall* was mainly a figment of Hitler's imagination, Army Group Centre's defensive measures were real enough. In early

August, they were able to blunt operations by Western and Kalinin Fronts and retake Smolensk. Soviet offensives in the north and at the centre unrolled against prepared German defences and difficult terrain. The gains were appreciably smaller than those in the southern theatre, where the prospect of a major breakthrough to the Dnieper, at the junction of two German Army Groups, now beckoned.

Late in September, Soviet armies driving over 150 miles (240 kilometres) to the west drew up to the Dnieper. Within a week, 23 bridgeheads dotted the Dnieper's western bank. During the night of 26 September, the Airborne Forces dropped 4,575 men in 296 aircraft sorties into the Bukrin bridgehead, an ambitious airborne operation marred by over-hasty improvisation and lack of unified command. The Soviet rush to the great river line became a frontal pursuit of the Germans complicated by dwindling supplies of fuel and ammunition. Astride the river, the Soviet command now planned the battle for the entire "Dnieper line". On 22 August, the *Stavka* approved the revised plan for the Smolensk operation further north. The final attack opened on 15 September, toppling German defensive bastions one by one. Smolensk, torched by retreating Germans, fell on 25 September. Soviet losses were heavy – the price the Soviet command paid for holding down 55 German divisions to prevent reinforcement reaching the southern wing, which the Red Army aimed to annihilate.

Early in October, the briefest lull settled across the Soviet–German front. Stalin planned to unleash an autumnal storm over two regional capitals: Minsk in Belorussia and Kiev in the Ukraine. Orders for the attack on Kiev had been issued and those for the liberation of Belorussia were readied. German military intelligence predicted, correctly, a powerful Soviet winter offensive, plus the chilling forecast that "the Soviet–Russian enemy will surpass Germany in terms of manpower, equipment and propaganda." Already the great dispersal of German forces, the very essence of Stalin's "war-shortening" strategy, had begun. Plans were in train for a massive winter attack to bring the Red Army to a line from which to launch decisive blows that would necessarily require full co-operation on the part of the Western allies. To this end, in late October, several Foreign Ministers met in Moscow to prepare for the "Big Three" conference to be attended by Roosevelt, Churchill and Stalin – it was to be held, at Stalin's insistence, in the Iranian capital,

Teheran. It was Stalin, flushed with victories, who came to dominate and domineer at Teheran at the end of November. He had taken great care on his way to Teheran to preserve himself from mishap. He travelled by train to Baku. At the airfield two aircraft waited, one for Stalin, piloted by a colonel-general, the other for officials piloted by a colonel. Stalin chose the colonel's aircraft, saying: "Colonel-generals don't often pilot aircraft".

On 6 November 1943, Kiev, "the mother of Russian cities", was cleared of enemy troops. The *Stavka* planned to smash in the "Dnieper line", hurling a great mass of men and tanks on Army Group South. The General Staff had completed the attack timetables for the winter offensive. Designed to destroy German forces at Leningrad, in Belorussia, the western Ukraine and the Crimea, the main attack was to be mounted in the southwestern theatre, the quicker to bring Soviet troops to the 1941 frontiers.

What Stalin wanted and pressed for at Teheran was a definite date for *Overlord*, the cross-Channel attack. He asked pointedly, "Who will command *Overlord*?" Churchill's proposals for a Third Front, a landing in southern France, attacking the German flank in the Balkans, were brutally shoved aside. Stalin fought to nail down *Overlord*. Did the British really believe in it or was this just "to keep the Russian quiet?" Resorting to ill-concealed blackmail, Stalin asserted that without *Overlord* materializing in May 1944, to coincide with Soviet offensive operations, the Red Army might falter and the Russians succumb to war-weariness. With *Overlord* on time, there would be no need "to take steps" to counter feelings of "isolation" in the Red Army. What Stalin could not win from Churchill he finally extracted at a lunch attended by all three Allied leaders: *Overlord* was timed for May 1944, enjoined as an Anglo–American decision and duly confirmed in the third plenary session.

The Teheran conference dispersed with a common decision formally agreed, though fundamental divisions shone through, glowing like hot coals. Stalin could congratulate himself: *Overlord* was now immovably anchored in the late spring of 1944, rival armies were diverted from his southern flank, Poland had been splintered, the Baltic states retained and a provisional territorial claim staked out in the Far East. Churchill departed Teheran in good order but was a prey to foreboding, seized with the urgent need to "do something with these bloody Russians".

THE END AT STALINGRAD: SURRENDER 1943

The battle of Stalingrad, which lasted from July 1942 to February 1943, cost the Red Army 1,129,619 men killed and wounded. While, before November, Stalin demanded that the city be held at all cost, Hitler now ruled out surrender by the German Sixth Army. The condition of the trapped German troops quickly worsened, from the grim to the ghastly, the dead and dying intermingled. Hopes of a successful German breakout faded as the Soviet outer "ring" was strengthened.

On 31 January, newly promoted Field Marshal Paulus surrendered, choosing captivity before suicide. At 1600 hours on 2 February, military operations ceased. It remained only to marshal prisoners and bury the dead.

Right
The Soviet 38th Motorized Rifle Brigade and 329th Engineer Battalion had blockaded the Univermak building, HQ of Sixth Army. On the morning of 31 January, Red Army Senior Lieutenants Ilchenko and Mezhirko entered the ruins. In the basement they presented a formal Soviet ultimatum and a demand for capitulation to a newly promoted Field Marshal von Paulus, seen here on the right.

Left
At noon on 31 January, Paulus was taken by car to General Mikhail Shumilov's 64th Army HQ and from there to Zavarykin Don Front command centre. There he was interrogated by General Rokossovskii, Colonel General Nikolai Voronov and interpreter Captain Nikolai Dyatlenko, who are shown seated from left to right. Paulus sits far right.

Above
These German officers are
packed and waiting to move
to Soviet prisoner of war
camps. Military operations
at Stalingrad had ended on
2 February, and the German
Sixth Army had ceased to
exist. The Red Army claimed
to have destroyed 22 Axis
divisions, plus 160 support
and re-enforcement units.

Above
A Stalingrad scene: massed German dead. In addition to the 91,000 prisoners of war, the battle of Stalingrad cost 147,000 German lives. Soviet losses at Stalingrad during the counter-offensive between 19 November 1942 and 2 February 1943 amounted to 485,735 killed, missing and wounded.

Right
German and Rumanian prisoners at Stalingrad. Two Rumanian armies, the 3rd and 4th, lost personnel and weapons equivalent to 16 of their 18 divisions, more than half the entire Rumanian 31 Divisions. Rumanian losses in the Stalingrad battle came to about 140,000 men, of whom 110,000 had been lost in the encirclement battle after 19 November 1942.

Opposite
One of the many endless columns formed by the 91,000 German prisoners of war taken by the Red Army at Stalingrad. They had a long and hazardous journey ahead of them: only 5,000 ever returned to Germany.

LENINGRAD'S "RAILWAY OF DEATH"

At 0930 hours on 12 January 1943, Operation *Iskra*, designed to pierce the German blockade of Leningrad, succeeded. Two Soviet Fronts, Leningrad and Volkhov, linked up to drive a seven-mile corridor through the German blockade lines. The 67th Army attacked eastward from inside the ring, while the 2nd Shock Army struck westward. The southern shore of Ladoga was swept clear of German troops and the Ladoga "ice road" still functioned. An 18-mile (29-kilometre) rail link was built along the new corridor. Shelled by German guns, "the railway of death" transported freight and coal, providing fuel for factories and power stations.

Right
Operation *Iskra* (Spark), the object of which was to pierce the Leningrad blockade, was finally successful in January 1943. Troops like these, from Lieutenant General Mikhail Dukhanov's 67th Army, had trained intensively since December 1942 in order to take on the formidable task of attacking across the ice of the Neva straight into German fixed defences.

Below
A shot-up Soviet T-34 tank at Nevskaya Dubrovka. The two Soviet Fronts, Leningrad and Volkhov, linked up on 18 January after heavy fighting against German strong points. The old fortress city Schlisselburg and the southern shore of Lake Ladoga were cleared of German troops.

Right
"FOR THE CITY OF LENIN, FORWARD!" This poster urges Soviet troops to rescue besieged, beleaguered Leningrad. Posters, radio and newspapers all played a vital role in sustaining both military and civilian morale. On 18 January, Radio Moscow declared the blockade broken.

Opposite
German prisoners being rounded up and searched by Red Army soldiers. In the foreground, two dead German soldiers – the one on the right is an SS trooper. Operation *Iskra* cost the Germans 13,000 men killed and 1,250 taken prisoner. Red Army losses amounted to 115,082 killed, missing or wounded.

BLUEPRINT FOR VICTORY

By 1943, all the resources of the Soviet Union were committed to the war effort: soldiers, scientists, women on the battle fronts, all sustaining the home front, the young and the old with the partisans.

Stalingrad proved that the Soviet Union could survive, and all efforts were now geared to winning. Tank designers developed new heavy tanks to overwhelm the Germans. The scientist Igor Kurchatov worked on nuclear fission. Women crewed tanks and heavy assault guns, became snipers and flew bombers and fighters. Forty-three per cent of Red Army doctors were women and female medics accompanied infantry assaults – their casualties were correspondingly heavy.

Right
Zhozef Kotin, Deputy Chief of the Soviet tank industry, was the brains behind the design and production of the Soviet heavy tanks, most notably the IS-2 (1943) with its 122-mm gun, the most powerful tank in the war. He also directed production of powerful assault guns, such as the SU-52.

Left
The physicist Igor Kurchatov was engaged on anti-mine defence and armour plate design in 1941–42, before being appointed director of atomic research. In 1943, Kurchatov held a seminar on nuclear fission and chain reaction, the first steps toward the Soviet atomic bomb.

Right
Nikolai Dukhov, tank designer, was closely associated with Kotin in the further development of Soviet heavy tanks. The main developments were steady improvements in fire-power and armour protection. Increasing armour thickness added to the immunity of the hull and the turret.

Left
Vyacheslav Malyshev, head of the Soviet tank industry. During the war, Malyshev's main responsibility was to ensure the production of the 100,000 tanks produced by Soviet industry. Most of these were medium tanks weighing 30 tons, such as the T-34 and T-34/85, which were designed to fight the mobile battle, while tanks over 45 tons were committed to breakthrough operations.

Right
Classic wartime
photograph: "The Red
Army political instructor
(*politruk*) continues to fight."

Left
The Red Army made much use of dogs on the battlefield. Dogs were trained to carry explosives in order to disable and, if possible, destroy German tanks. Here they are being used to assist with the evacuation of the wounded.

Right
The traditional image of the "nurse" had difficulty surviving the carnage of mechanized warfare and hand-to-hand fighting. Losses among young women medics, such as those shown here, who served with the rifle battalions, were second only to those of the fighting troops themselves. One 16-year-old front-line medic serving with a rifle company flung into hand-to-hand fighting said, "That was awful … it isn't for human beings."

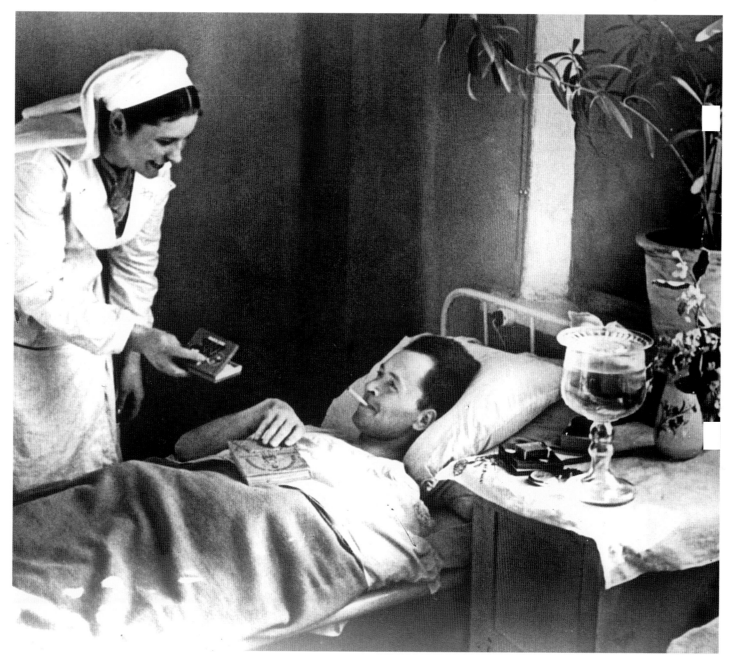

Above
The totals for Red Army
wounded and sick during
the Great Patriotic War vary
between 18 and 22 million.
At least 15 million men
and women were wounded
and a further three million
became sick. The nurse
in the picture was very
probably trained in a
crash programme organized
by the Red Cross and
Trade Union organizations
to work on hospital trains
or in military hospitals.

Overleaf
Fuel and ammunition took
greater priority than rations
in the Red Army, although
theoretical daily norms
included: bread, flour
macaroni, meat, fish,
potatoes, vegetables, tea
and salt. The best efforts
were made to supply
at least porridge or hot
soup, as in this photograph.
Perhaps the most appreciated
daily ration was 4 oz
(100 grams) of vodka!

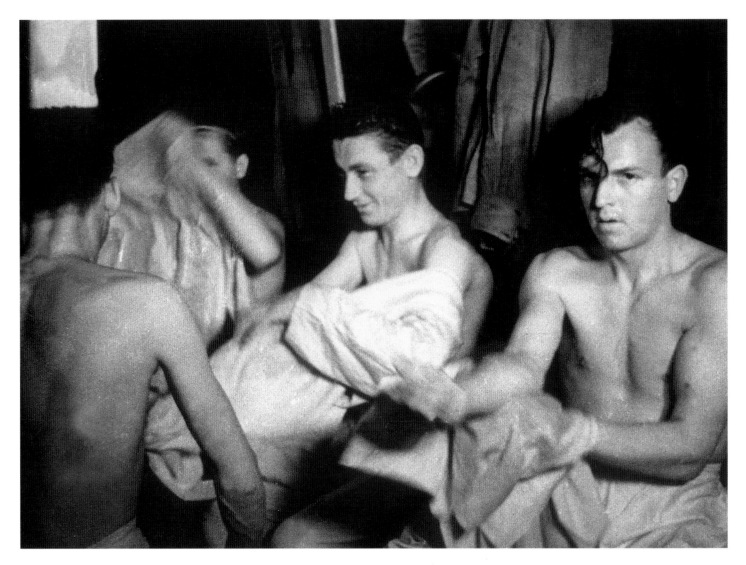

Above
The bath house, the great luxury
for every soldier. Some units had
women who ran "laundry units"
with great efficiency and stern
discipline – some of these
laundresses became very well
known. Front-line soldiers received
clean uniforms and fresh clothing
whenever possible.

Above
Dmitrii Shoshtakovich's *Leningrad Symphony* was first performed here in Moscow. A powerful work, its first movement depicts the German invasion of Russia. The emotional impact of the war and the crises it produced also inspired striking artistic works by Boris Pasternak, Aleksei Surkov – the "soldiers' poet" – and Ilya Ehrenburg.

Right
These Red Army soldiers are being decorated, in the field, for bravery. Such occasions were used to enhance morale, as were ceremonial presentations of Communist Party membership cards.

Left
Soviet war correspondents often became celebrities, and this was certainly true of Boris Tseitlin, Roman Karmen and Konstantin Simonov, pictured here (left to right) at Vyazma. For some, celebrity was fatal. Karmen was already a well-known film producer and screen writer, directing several front-line film crews. Simonov spent the entire war at the front and eventually became a lieutenant colonel. He worked as special war correspondent of the military newspaper *Red Star*.

Above
The woman in the tank turret,
Mariya Oktyabrskaya, Hero of the
Soviet Union, died of wounds on
15 March 1944. Her husband
was killed at the front in 1941.
She used her own money to
purchase a tank and trained as a
driver and mechanic. With her
tank, she joined the 26th Guards
Tank Brigade, the 2nd Guards Tank
Army, Western Front and rose to
the rank of Guards Sergeant.

Right
Young women especially
excelled as snipers.
Here, two young would-be
snipers are training
on the Mosin-Nagant
Model 1891/30 rifle
with Model PE Telescope.

Below
As well as being excellent
snipers, Soviet women
established a unique
reputation for themselves
as fighter and bomber pilots.
Three women's air regiments
were established, among
them the 46th Guards
Women's Night Light
Bomber Regiment.
Here, the 46th Regiment
Commander Captain E.E.
Bershanskaya and Regiment
Commissar E. Ya. Rachkovich
are seen next to their U-2
biplane after a sortie.

Right
The award of Hero of the Soviet Union went posthumously to 30 women air crew, an appreciable number. In addition to flying the U-2, women pilots such as these flew Pe-2 bombers with the 125th Guards Day Bomber Regiment. Colonel Valentina Grizodubova flew 200 sorties on bombing raids or supporting partisans.

Left
Women snipers from the Red Army, such as the one pictured, came from the Central Women's School for Sniper Training. The school was commanded by a regular Red Army woman officer, N.P. Chegodaeva, a veteran of the Spanish Civil War. It turned out 1,061 women snipers and 407 instructors. The graduates killed some 12,000 German soldiers.

These decorated women snipers had reason to be cheerful – they had so far survived. Their fates were often sealed in deadly sniper duels. One captured German officer asked to see the skilled marksman who had killed so many of his men – he was told this was impossible because the "marksman" was a young woman, Sasha Shlyakova, who had herself just been killed in a sniper duel.

Women flight mechanics working on the engine of a U-2 biplane. The women's night bomber regiments carried out night raids over the German lines in their slow-moving, unarmed, open-cockpit biplanes. On the ground, young women armourers struggled to load bomb racks for five or six sorties each night before dawn.

Women played a vital role on the home front. Those not subject to the call-up joined home-guard units, the guard and security units organized to deal with enemy parachutists, spies, deserters, and "panic mongers". Some, just like the young woman seen here on the roof of a Leningrad building, joined the fire service, itself a very hazardous assignment.

KURSK: CLASH OF ARMOUR

In 1943, the Red Army re-organized and re-armed, ready to meet Operation *Zitadelle*, the massive German armoured assault on the Soviet salient at Kursk. *Zitadelle* used 2,700 tanks and 1,800 aircraft and was designed by Hitler to bring final victory. Postponed once, *Zitadelle* opened on 5 July 1943 with two powerful German attacks on the northern and southern faces of the salient. The Red Army was ready and waiting with the largest strategic reserve it had yet assembled. Amid great armoured jousts, German attacks from the west and south were held off, and *Zitadelle* was smashed beyond recovery. On 3 August, an enormous, unexpected, Soviet counter-offensive unrolled, striking north and south, recovering Orel and closing on Belgorod-Kharkov.

Below
German units moving up to the battle of Kursk. This image shows the contrasting styles of the German army in Russia: horse-drawn transport, and even the bicycle, which may have been used by foot-sore German soldiers; and on the right, the fearsome Pz Kfw VI Tiger tank, weighing 55 tons and armed with an 88-mm 36L/56 gun.

Below
A Soviet tank factory in 1943. The challenge posed by the appearance of the German Tiger tank demanded not only increases in output from Soviet tank factories but also improvements in quality. The mainstay Soviet medium tank, the T-34, was in the process of being upgunned to emerge as the T-34/85. New, heavy tanks designed by Kotin and Dukhov were also on their way.

Above
During the fighting for the Kursk salient, the Central Front was commanded by General K. Rokossovskii, seen here (centre) with Major General Konstantin Telegin and Major General Maksimenko. The German Ninth Army attacked the Central Front on 5 July, but was unable to make deep penetration into the massive Soviet defences. On 12 July, Rokossovskii halted the German forces in their tracks and the Ninth Army began to withdraw on 14 July.

Above

A significant portrait of Stalin, who was elevated in 1943 to Marshal of the Soviet Union. Step by step, Stalin mounted the military ladder: member of the *Stavka*, 23 June 1941; head of the *Stavka*, 10 July 1941; chairman of the State Defence Committee (GKO), from 30 June 1941 to 4 September 1945; July Defence Commissar from 19 July 1941 to March 1947; and Supreme Commander Soviet Armed Forces from August 1941 to September 1945. In 1945 Stalin was invested with the title of Generalissimus, a rare distinction.

Right

Two Soviet commanders destined to become rivals: General Ivan Konev – Steppe Front commander at Kursk (centre) – and newly promoted Marshal Zhukov (right), receiving a report from General Ivan Managarov, 51st Army. Marshal Zhukov now had the management of the "Belgorod-Kharkov operation", code-named Operation *Rumyantsev*. On 5 August, Soviet tanks were deep in German defences and Belgorod fell the same day. On 28 August, Konev liberated Kharkov. Thus ended the battle of Kursk.

Left
The spoils of war. Marshal Zhukov and Colonel General Nikolai Voronov, commander of Red Army Artillery, (front row left to right) inspect a German Tiger tank captured at Kursk. Kursk was the scene of the greatest tank battles of the Second World War.

Right
. At Kursk, the Red Army constructed an elaborate defensive system. The core of each Soviet defensive position was its anti-tank defences, organized into a network covered by the interlocking fires of multiple anti-tank guns, as seen here. Firing over open sights, Soviet guns were often left with only one or two men alive, while "anti-tank squads" attacked tanks with explosive charges.

Left
At Kursk, the Red Army committed more than a million men, more than 3,275 tanks and 25,000 guns and mortars. Soviet riflemen like these had to hold off "tank fists" and German assault infantry supported by dive-bombers and heavy artillery fire. Soviet losses at Kursk amounted to 177,847 men killed, missing or wounded.

Right
The battle of Kursk reached its crisis between 11–12 July. At Prokhorovka, more than a thousand tanks engaged in a battle that saw II SS Panzer Corps penetrate Voronezh Front defences. Lieutenant General Pavel Rotmistrov (right), commander of the 5th Guards Tank Army, counter-attacked. His tanks charged across open terrain, closing on German tanks. Rotmistrov lost 400 of his 800 tanks; the Germans lost 320 tanks and self-propelled guns.

Below
Forward To Orel: aerial view of the high wheat fields. On 12 July, the Red Army opened its strategic offensive, beginning with Operation *Kutuzov* against the Orel salient, just north of the Kursk salient. This Soviet attack caught the Germans by surprise. Ultimately, three Soviet Fronts, the Western, Bryansk and Central, launched the main attack. Lieutenant General Pavel Rybalko's 3rd Guards Tank Army penetrated German defences on 14 July.

Overleaf (pages 160–161)
5 August 1943. Orel is free! After very heavy fighting, the 3rd Guards Tank Army entered the city.

Following page (page 162)
Another famous photograph: the victory parade in Orel, August 1943.

Above

A galaxy of talent: Marshal Aleksandr Vasilevskii (centre), Chief of the Soviet General Staff, a brilliant strategic planner, together with Zhukov, *Stavka* co-ordinator at Kursk, at this time with the Southern Front. To the right, Aleksandr Novikov, commander of the Soviet Air Force, also *Stavka* co-ordinator at Kursk. Novikov had reorganized the Soviet Air Force, introducing "air armies", aviation corps and divisions. Also pictured (second from left): General Yakov Kreizer, commander of the 51st Army.

Right

A German cemetery at Kursk. The Red Army set German losses at Kursk at 70,000 men killed, 2,952 tanks, 195 assault guns, 844 field guns destroyed, 1,392 aircraft and over 5,000 lorries. Losses in individual Panzers were severe: the 3rd Panzer was left with 30 tanks out of 300 and the 17th Panzer (after Prokhorovka) with only 60 tanks. In German infantry divisions, companies were reduced to 40 men and regiments were not much stronger.

THE RUSSIAN LIBERATION MOVEMENT?

Red Army Lieutenant General Andrei Vlasov, Commander of the 2nd Shock Army, Volkhov Front, was taken prisoner by the Germans in July 1942. During a failed attempt to break the Leningrad blockade, his army had been surrounded and finally forced to surrender. Vlasov was persuaded to join the Germans, organize an anti-Stalin Russian Liberation movement and form Soviet prisoners of war into the Russian Liberation Army (ROA). The Soviet authorities made strenuous efforts to discredit and infiltrate "the Vlasov movement", denouncing Vlasov as a traitor and tool of the Germans. What Lieutenant General Vlasov needed most, a change in the barbarous German occupation policies, never materialized.

Above

"Volunteer!" Depicted in this Russian Liberation Army poster is a recruit to the anti-Stalinist, anti-Bolshevik military force that was raised with German support from Soviet prisoners of war. Stalin took the threat from the "Vlasovites" seriously, as both Russians and non-Russian nationalities joined the Germans.

Right

"The Caucasus will be free!" Almost 800,000 Russians and non-Russians briefly joined the Germans. None was "freed" and they paid dearly for their collaboration. The Muslim peoples of the northern Caucasus were "liquidated". Crimean Tartars, Kalmuks, the Chechen-Ingush and others were exiled to Siberia. The same fate awaited the inhabitants of the German Volga republic.

THE DRIVE TO THE DNIEPER

At the end of August 1943, the Red Army summer offensive unrolled across a vast front from north to south. Stalin planned to hurl Soviet armies on to the Dnieper, recovering the Donbas industries and the east Ukrainian breadlands.

Five Soviet Fronts were concentrated in the southwest: 2,633,000 men, 2,400 tanks along with Ukrainian partisans were assigned a specific role in Soviet operations. At the end of September, Soviet armies drove 150 miles (240 kilometres) to the west, drew up to the Dnieper river and established 23 bridgeheads. In the Crimea, German forces faced complete isolation. On 6 November, Kiev, "mother of Russian cities", was cleared of German troops.

Above
Soviet armoured columns. Manstein thought Soviet armies in the southern part of the Kursk salient too badly damaged to attack. On 16 July, however, the *Stavka* had ordered General Konev's Steppe Front to become fully operational. On 3 August, an enormous Soviet attack with armoured columns on the move unrolled against German forces in the Belgorod–Kharkov area.

Above
Army General Nikolai Vatutin, Commander of the 1st Ukrainian Front (right) and Lieutenant General Nikita Khrushchev (left) photographed on the Bukrin bridgehead. Vatutin's tanks had reached the Dnieper north and south of Kiev. Of the 40 bridgeheads over the Dnieper, the most useful was at Veliki Bukrin, just south of Kiev. To reinforce the bridgehead, Vatutin decided to use airborne troops.

Above
The price of collaboration in Kiev,
1943: the public hanging of
"killers and provocateurs".

THE TURNING POINT: TEHERAN 1943

Between 28 November and 1 December 1943, the "Big Three" met in Teheran, which was Stalin's choice of venue. The agenda was primarily military, the issue being the Russian demand for a definite date for the proposed cross-Channel attack. At the outset, Stalin promised Russian entry into the war against Japan, much to the satisfaction of America. Churchill's attempt to press for a "Mediterranean strategy" was forcibly rejected by Stalin. The Americans and Russians were united on strategy, and Churchill appeared "deliberately obstructionist". Stalin won a confirmed timing for Operation *Overlord*, held rival armies off his southern flank, splintered Poland, kept the Baltic States in his grasp and staked a claim in the Far East.

Above
At Teheran, on 29 November, Churchill, in Air Commodore uniform, presented Marshal Stalin with the specially made Sword of Stalingrad, inscribed "Gift of King George VI", as a token of the homage of the British people. Stalin replied briefly, kissed the scabbard and handed the sword to Marshal Voroshilov. Here, Voroshilov shows the sword to President Roosevelt (seated centre).

1944

LIBERATION, CONQUEST

At the beginning of 1944, marked out as "the year of the ten decisive blows", the Red Army first struck on the northern and southern wings of the Soviet–German front. With the piercing of the blockade, life had become less nightmarish in Leningrad but it still remained dangerous, cramped and hard: unbroken privation, unending work, the narrow supply corridor raked by German guns. The planned Soviet offensive to lift the blockade involved three Fronts: Leningrad, Volkhov and 2nd Baltic. The aims were the destruction of the German Eighteenth Army, Leningrad's tormentor, and the elimination of the Sixteenth Army. This would clear the entire Leningrad *oblast*, preparing the way for a general offensive into the Baltic states.

On 15 January 1944, three thousand guns and heavy mortars opened a massive bombardment, firing over 200,000 rounds in 100 minutes. Four days later, Soviet troops captured at heavy cost over 100 heavy siege guns, which only hours before had been shelling Leningrad. Retreating German units were harassed by partisan brigades. By 20 January, the Red Army's double breakthrough was accomplished. The German Eighteenth Army no longer held a firm front. Though the planned great encirclement failed to materialize as the Eighteenth Army fought its way out of the trap, on 27 January 1944 Leningrad was freed and the Moscow–Leningrad rail link reopened. Nine hundred days of gruesome martyrdom were ended. Soviet troops had already crossed the Estonian frontier. As Germany's hold on the northern theatre weakened substantially, alarm bells began ringing in Finland.

The first blow had been delivered. Stalin now unleashed a massive offensive designed to destroy German armies in the south. The prelude was the reduction of the Korsun salient, its blunted nose pressed up to the Dnieper. In a battle of unbelievable ferocity, in which Soviet tanks finally ploughed into the column of retreating Germans, the salient was eliminated. Further south, German defences were overwhelmed at Krivoi Rog and Nikopol. The lower bend of the Don was swept clean, opening the way for a full-scale attack on the Crimea.

The bloody German sacrifice at Korsun had delayed but not frustrated a pending Soviet offensive. Soviet armies regrouped and Stalin signed directives for the massive March offensive in southern Russia, which involved four Fronts. A fifth was detached for the attack on the Crimea. The *Stavka* proposed to commit all six Soviet tank armies in the Ukraine. Marshal Zhukov planned to drive southward, first isolating the First Panzer Army and cutting German links with Poland. The offensive would also develop in a westerly direction. Badly mauled, the First Panzer escaped Zhukov's trap, but at the end of March, little of the Ukraine was in German hands. Zhukov's right flank rested on Galicia, the left pressed on the Bukovina. Advance guards had reached the borders of sub-Carpathian Ruthenia, Czechoslovakia's doorstep. Koniev had forced the Prut, threatening Rumania. In early April, Odessa was liberated. Malinovskii positioned himself for an advance into Rumania. Like the Finns in the north, the Rumanians looked for escape routes. The roof had already fallen in on "Greater Rumania". Hitler's response was to order German military occupation of Rumania and Hungary.

At the end of April 1944, the Soviet General Staff completed the full operational plan for the coming summer offensive. Stalin permitted northwestern and western theatres to move temporarily on to the defensive; other fronts would "consolidate", but no commander "must rush on to the defensive". The Red Army's decisive campaign would involve feinting on the flanks in the northwest and south. The mass of offensive power was aimed at the centre in Belorussia: Operation *Bagration*, designed to destroy the last great concentration of German strength in Russia – Army Group Centre – and blast a path into the Reich itself.

In its final form, Operation *Bagration*, named after the famous Russian general who was killed fighting Napoleon's army in Russia, was to open with simultaneous attacks on the German flanks at Vitebsk and Bobruisk, destroying German troops at Moghilev and clearing the road to Minsk. Once west of Minsk, the Red Army would cut the German escape route, trapping Army Group Centre and destroying it piecemeal. The *Stavka* also planned an operation to knock Finland out of the war and, in the south, to destroy German Army Group North Ukraine. Here Koniev proposed to split German forces, hurling one part back into Poland, pushing the other back to the Carpathians, to bring his 1st Ukrainian Front to the Vistula.

Meanwhile, Stalin waited for the launch of the Anglo–American cross-Channel attack, Operation *Overlord*. The coming Soviet offensive corresponded to Stalin's commitment given at the Teheran conference. Now Stalin waited for the Western allies to meet theirs. On 9 June 1944, a foretaste of what was to come, the Red Army opened its offensive on Finland. While assisting Anglo–American deception measures to confuse the Germans over time and place for "D-day", the Soviet command carried through a hugely successful deception operation of its own, a double bluff in its southern theatre. The German command was fully persuaded that the coming offensive would unroll in Galicia, striking Army Group North Ukraine. Army Group Centre would be subject only to diversionary attacks. German reserves went to North Ukraine. Hitler categorically forbade Army Group Centre to pull back in spite of identifying massive Soviet movement. Soviet tank armies appeared to be deployed against Army Group North Ukraine.

Precisely on the third anniversary of the Wehrmacht's surprise attack on the Soviet Union, 22 June 1944, the Red Army unleashed its firestorm over Army Group Centre. The huge Soviet offensive was staggered, unrolling from north to south, persuading the German command these were only holding attacks. As Soviet assault armies closed on Vitebsk from the northwest, the Third Panzer Army faced a critical situation. The German Fourth and Ninth Armies were under sustained attack. Once Rokossovskii launched his double attack on Bobruisk, the Ninth Army's situation became near-catastrophic. Three German armies were being sliced away from each other. At the end of June, the first phase of *Bagration* ended with the fall of Vitebsk, Orsha, Moghilev and Bobruisk. German armies had lost 900 tanks, 130,000 men were killed and 66,000 taken prisoner. On 3 July, Minsk fell, trapping the Fourth Army and shattering Army Group Centre. The Red Army had achieved its greatest single success on the Eastern Front, greater even than Stalingrad. It could now ram the weakened German centre back to the Vistula and the East Prussian frontier, threaten the isolation of the Baltic states and menace German positions in the southeast. The German strategic front had been well and truly breached.

The Soviet command now consummated its "double bluff". The Soviet offensive the German command had earlier anticipated now materialized. Marshal Koniev's 1st Ukrainian Front, the most powerful in the Red Army, smashed into Army Group North Ukraine, splitting it in two: the Fourth Panzer Army fell back on the Vistula while the First Panzer withdrew southwestward toward the Carpathians. At the end of July, Soviet armies had advanced to the Vistula, deploying on the eastern approaches to Warsaw.

Throughout August and September, the German Army fought savagely to destroy the Polish insurgency in Warsaw, the Warsaw Rising. Opposite the blazing Polish capital, on the eastern bank of the Vistula river, the Red Army stood immobile. Bitterly opposed to the rising, Stalin strenuously resisted attempts to bring outside aid to the desperate Poles. At the beginning of October 1944, fire-blackened, ruined Warsaw still lay ahead of the stationary Red Army. Three hundred miles (480 kilometres) to the south, an anti-German rising in Slovakia occurred almost simultaneously with the Warsaw Rising, only for "Free Slovakia" to suffer the same tragic, bloody fate as the Warsaw insurgents.

The defeat of Army Group Centre, Soviet bridgeheads over the Vistula and the push to the outskirts of Warsaw had advanced Soviet armies some 350 miles (560 kilometres) along the Berlin axis. In the north, the Red Army had pounded the Finns into submission. At the other end of the Soviet–German Front, late in August, the Red Army launched a high-speed attack into Rumania. On 23 August 1944, Rumania defected from the Axis, a coup that stranded German forces and threatened the entire German defensive system in the southeastern theatre, exposing the route into Hungary, the road to Yugoslavia and Bulgaria and the gateway to Czechoslovakia and Austria to Soviet armies. Bulgaria succumbed to panic. The prospect of Soviet control fastened over southeastern Europe disturbed Churchill. He seized the opportunity at his 9 October meeting with Stalin, amid "an extraordinary atmosphere of goodwill", to attempt to "settle our affairs in the Balkans". Mutually acceptable outcomes did not quickly materialize, although the Soviet Union disengaged from Greece.

At the end of July, the entire German front in the north was threatened with collapse as key positions fell: Dvinsk, Shaulyai and Narva. Soviet armies now rushed for the Gulf of Riga. Army Group North was completely cut off; its last land communication with the German Army on the Eastern Front and its rear in East Prussia were severed by rapid Soviet tank thrusts. Plans were afoot for a massive concentric attack on Riga designed to isolate Army Group North for good. Riga fell on 13 October. After ten weeks the Red Army had succeeded in slicing Army Group North away from East Prussia. Save for Courland, the pre-1941 Soviet frontiers were now fully restored everywhere. Finland had surrendered, the Baltic states were virtually cleared, East Prussia was penetrated and bridgeheads had been established on the Vistula. Further south, the Red Army was fighting close to Budapest.

On 28 October 1944, the Soviet General Staff prepared plans for the final campaign of the war: the Soviet invasion of Hitler's Reich, a campaign unleashing men in millions and their machines in many thousands. The 1944 offensives had succeeded beyond expectations. The greatest depth of penetration, 750 miles (1200 kilometres), was reached in the southeastern theatre. All German Army Groups had suffered drastic losses by Soviet reckoning: 96 divisions and 24 brigades, 219 divisions badly mauled, more than one-and-a-half million men, 6,700 tanks and over 12,000 aircraft lost.

"We deserve the right to enter Berlin" was Stalin's sentiment exactly. He nominated a senior Soviet operational commander and designated specific Front forces to capture Berlin, but he reserved the key role of "co-ordinator" exclusively for himself. Within days, Stalin confirmed that the 1st Belorussian Front would operate in the "Berlin strategic zone" with Marshal Zhukov in command. The General Staff now grappled with a serious problem. The battle for Berlin would be decided on the Warsaw–Poznan axis and the Silesian axis, but heavy German resistance would be encountered here. A radical alternative was to use the southern fronts in a deep penetration aimed at the Reich, passing through Budapest, Bratislava, Vienna. That option was rejected as the German grip on Hungary tightened and fighting for Budapest took a desperate turn, leading to a ghastly, lengthy siege.

Stalin ordered all fronts to move temporarily on to the defensive while the "Berlin planning" was revised. At this point, Anglo-American and Soviet armies were roughly equidistant from Berlin. In the west, 74 German divisions with 1,600 tanks faced 87 Allied divisions supported by 6,000 tanks, while in the east, the Wehrmacht deployed three million men and some 4,000 tanks. The General Staff drew immediate conclusions about "the race for Berlin". For the Red Army, the "central sector" was critical, affording the most direct route into Germany, but here German resistance would be fiercest. To weaken the German centre, the Red Army must exert maximum pressure on the flanks: in Hungary, Austria and East Prussia. A powerful thrust into Budapest and against Vienna was to be accompanied by a simultaneous attack on Königsberg.

At the beginning of November 1944, the General Staff plan was complete, specifying that within 45 days the German war machine could be smashed by offensive operations reaching to a depth of 350–400 miles (480–640 kilometres) in a two-stage operation, though without "operational pauses". The first stage would take 15 days, the second 30. For this final apocalyptic battle, the Red Army fielded over six million men, 13,000 tanks, 15,000 aircraft, 55 field armies, six tank armies, 13 air armies and no fewer than 500 rifle divisions. Hitler scoffed, "It's all an enormous bluff".

LENINGRAD FREED: 26 JANUARY

The year of the "ten decisive blows", 1944, opened with the freeing of Leningrad from blockade. Life had become less nightmarish after the penetration of the blockade in January 1943, but remained dangerous, cramped and hard. The Soviet offensive involved three Fronts – Leningrad, Volkhov and the 2nd Baltic – its aim: to eliminate the German Eighteenth Army, Leningrad's tormentor, and the Sixteenth, thus freeing the entire Leningrad *oblast* and opening the way into the Baltic states. Although the planned Soviet encirclement failed to materialize, on 26 January the Leningrad–Moscow railway was cleared, and this was followed by Stalin's permission to declare the blockade ended, terminating 900 days of death and privation.

Left
At 0920 hours on 15 January 1944, the Red Army offensive aimed at Leningrad opened after an initial heavy bombardment. Soviet troops had to hack their way through German defences. The infantry became locked in hundreds of separate engagements, such as the one in progress in this image captured in Gatchina (Krasnogvardeisk). The soldier on the left is firing from a PPSh-41 submachine gun.

Above
Soviet artillery spotters observing and correcting fire in the Leningrad offensive. A good half of heavy-calibre guns firing at German defences in the breakthrough sector were assigned to Major General Nikolai Simonyak's 30th Guards Corps, 42nd Army. Simonyak's Corps made the best progress on the first day, driving 4,000 yards (3,600 metres) into German trenches.

Above
Gatchina is free! By 20 January,
the Red Army had achieved a
double breakthrough at
Leningrad. The first phase of the
Soviet offensive was now
drawing to a close. With fresh
armies committed, the Red Army
offensive was unfolding across a
broad front running from the Gulf
of Finland to Lake Ilmen.

Right
The divisions of the German Eighteenth Army no longer held a firm front. As the Soviet offensive rolled forward, defensive actions were fought at junctions, small towns, high ground and roads. Wherever possible, German rear-guards fought powerful, skilful actions to deflect the Soviet advance. The cost is vividly illustrated here: weary, harried German troops conduct a fighting retreat.

Above
On 12 February, the Red
Army captured Luga, a vital
junction in the German rear,
cutting the German escape
route to the southwest.
Troops from General Ivan
Fedyuninskii's 2nd Shock
Army, pictured, had reached
the Narva river north
and south of Narva itself.
The *Stavka* ordered Narva to
be captured by 17 February.

Right
One by one, German
bastions in the north
toppled. German
rear-guards, like those
pictured here, fought
to keep escape routes
open. Regiments were
covered by battalions,
battalions by companies,
which fought in isolation
or with improvised
battle groups.

A "FLICK OF THE STALINGRAD WHIP": 1944

Southeast of Kiev, two German corps held a huge salient sloping toward the Dnieper around Korsun-Shevchenkovskii, the boundary between the First Panzer and Eighth Army. This was all that remained of Hitler's much-vaunted "Dnieper Line", and the German salient was ripe for encirclement. At dawn on 24 January, Konev attacked using 13 rifle and three cavalry divisions to reduce the "Korsun pocket". Trapped German divisions tried desperately to fight their way out, making a final breakout on 17 February. Once in open country, the Germans were savagely attacked by Soviet tanks and Cossacks, a "flick of the Stalingrad whip" that cost the Germans 55,000 dead and wounded.

Left
Stalin demanded the speedy "liquidation" of the German forces trapped at Korsun before relief could arrive. General Werner Stemmermann and his remaining units determined on a final breakout. At 0200 hours on 17 February, as a blizzard raged, Stemmermann's troops finished their last supplies and destroyed guns and lorries, leaving scenes like this one. There was no place in the columns for the wounded, who were killed where they lay. As the German column moved into open country, Soviet tanks charged straight into it and Cossacks hunted down and massacred fleeing Germans.

Right
The Germans claimed 30,000 men escaped Soviet encirclement. Here, Field Marshal Manstein (second from left) greets soldiers who broke out of the Soviet trap. The Red Army claimed 55,000 Germans killed and 18,000 taken prisoner. For this success, Stalin promoted Konev to Marshal of the Soviet Union.

Opposite
The beginning of Konev's famous "mud offensive" reducing the German salient, pressed up to the Dnieper at Korsun. The Soviet offensive against the beleaguered Germans began on 26 January 1944. Konev unleashed a savage, remorseless attack that hacked the defences to pieces. By 10 February, Konev's assault divisions were closing in on Korsun.

SEVASTOPOL REVENGED

The final offensive of the Red Army's winter campaign was launched against the German Seventeenth Army in the Crimea, which had long been isolated from the main body of German troops. Reduction of this German strongly fortified Crimean redoubt was assigned to Tolbukhin's 4th Ukrainian Front, which would attack across the Perekop Isthmus and the Sivash lagoons and drive on against Simferopol and Sevastopol. On 5 May, striking in the north along the Mackenzie Heights, Soviet forces began the assault on Sevastopol. Only four days later, Sevastopol was in Soviet hands and the Seventeenth Army was virtually annihilated. Soviet revenge for 1942 was as swift as it was complete.

Right
Soviet marines from the
Black Sea Fleet lead an assault
party in the fighting for
Sevastopol. Russian infantrymen
had pushed their way into the
outskirts of Sevastopol and
pressed on to the main railway
station, where they engaged in
heavy street-fighting.

Above
The Black Sea Fleet takes
possession of its principal
base, Sevastopol.
The capture of Sevastopol
had taken the Germans
250 days in 1941–1942.
The Red Army and the
Red Navy reclaimed the
city in a matter of hours.

Left
Soviet infantry in the assault
on Sevastopol. Early in
May, Soviet preparations
for the final assault on
Sevastopol were almost
complete and Stalin was
demanding rapid action
and immediate results.
The Soviet assault opened
on 5 May, with infantry
advancing in the face
of German heavy fire.

Above
Amid the ruins of Sevastopol, Soviet infantry mop up. On 9 May, the city had fallen. The next day, Tolbukhin reported the victory to Stalin, who immediately demanded that the Crimea be cleared of all German troops within the next 24 hours. The Germans made a last stand at Kherson, where Soviet infantry, artillery and aircraft attacked the trapped German regiments. At noon on 12 May, 25,000 German troops surrendered.

Above
Sunbathing against a backdrop
of the ruins of Sevastopol.

THE BATTLE FOR BELORUSSIA: JUNE–JULY 1944

On 19 June, partisans attacked rail links, opening the battle for Belorussia. This was the prelude to the destruction of Army Group Centre, which had been left incomplete by Zhukov since 1941–42. Russian deception confused the Germans over the main Russian objective. By 20 June, the Red Army had concentrated 166 rifle divisions, 1,254,000 men and 2,715 tanks for the attack. Three years to the day from the date of the Wehrmacht's *Barbarossa*, 22 June 1944, Operation *Bagration* was launched. One week later Vitebsk, Orsha and Moghilev had fallen, and the German defensive system was split wide open. The Germans lost 130,000 men and a further 105,000 men from the Fourth Army became trapped when Minsk was captured.

Below
German dead in Vitebsk.
On 25 June, Soviet troops fought their way into Vitebsk. The next day, the German garrison surrendered, leaving 20,000 dead. One force of 8,000 German troops, while fighting its way out of Vitebsk, was surrounded once again and wiped out. The Red Army was doing to the German Army in 1944 what the German Army had done to the Red Army in 1941.

Opposite
The rout of Army Group Centre in Belorussia was the Wehrmacht's gravest defeat in the East. In one week, three German Armies had lost over 130,000 men and 900 tanks, with a further 66,000 men taken prisoner.
On 17 July, the Red Army marched 57,000 German prisoners of war, generals and officers at their head, through the streets of Moscow.
This was to demonstrate to some sceptical elements that Soviet victories in Belorussia had been hard won.

Right
Ukrainian partisans operated under the immediate auspices of the Red Army and, in the winter of 1944, came under direct Red Army control. Major General Sidor Kovpak (seen here) had built up a considerable guerrilla force since 1941–42 and organized the Carpathian raid in 1943. In January 1944, his partisan units were combined to form the 1st Ukrainian Kovpak Division.

Left
The National Committee of "Free Germany" (NK), founded in July 1943, was composed of anti-Nazi German prisoners of war. A later organization, the "League of German Officers" (BDO), included a number of German generals taken prisoner at Stalingrad, among them Field Marshal Paulus, seen in this photograph pointing at prisoners' garden produce.

Right
German prisoners of war at work in Russia. According to Soviet figures, 3,604,800 Germans were killed, wounded or missing and 3,576,300 German prisoners were taken. Of these, 442,100 died in captivity and 2,910,400 returned to Germany.

Below
An aerial view of the ruins of Minsk, where nearly all factories and public buildings had been destroyed by the Germans and the majority of houses had been burned down. Some large official buildings and 19 out of 332 industrial plants survived only because they had been rapidly de-mined: 4,000 delayed-action bombs remained to be defused. On 3 July, with the capture of Minsk, the Red Army trapped 105,000 men of the German Fourth Army. More than 40,000 died attempting to escape.

Above
A Red Army soldier feeds an infant girl he
has found in a liberated village in
Belorussia. The retreating Germans had
turned most of Belorussia into a "scorched
earth zone". Over a million houses had
been destroyed and hundreds of villages
had been burned down, the inhabitants
murdered or deported.

Above
This farmer and his family are returning to
their home after the German occupation
ended. Many families fled to the forests or
to the protection of the partisans. What
awaited them was more hardship. The
Germans had destroyed what harvested
crops there were, had ordered the winter
crops to be ploughed in and had
prevented spring sowing.

Right
Revenge, retribution? Public hanging of a *starosta*, an elder or village headman, who was responsible for villages or other small population centres. The German Army appointed only individuals from the local population to positions of authority. Their political reliability was usually checked by the Gestapo or German field security.

Left
The retreating German armies employed special machines to destroy crops and rip up railway lines. The machine shown here rips up sleepers and distorts rails as it moves along the line.

Right
The dam at Dnepropetrovsk. Dnepropetrovsk's hydroelectric power station, completed in 1932, the pride and joy of Soviet industrialization, was blown up by the Russians in 1941. Now, with the Germans in retreat, it was time to rebuild and restore the installation.

THE WARSAW RISING

After the German rout in Belorussia, the Red Army reached the Vistula; ahead lay Warsaw. On 1 August, anticipating Allied or Soviet help, 37,600 Polish insurgents, nearly all from the Polish Home Army, launched Operation *Tempest* against the Germans in Warsaw. The German counter-attack was ferocious, employing SS units and the criminal, anti-partisan Kaminsky Brigade. In five days, 40,000 Poles were shot. Allied aircraft attempted to drop aid to the insurgents; Soviet airdrops began only on 1 September.

The Poles fought on for 63 days, losing 15,000 Home Army soldiers and between 200,000 and 250,000 civilians, compared with German losses of 17,000 men.

Above
Warsaw was the scene of two risings against the Nazis. On 19 April 1943, German troops attacked the Warsaw ghetto. The Jews of the ghetto had realized that death and extermination were inevitable, but decided to fight. It took almost a month for German troops and SS units commanded by Jürgen Stroop to suppress it. The second Warsaw rising began on 1 August 1944.

Left
The Poles' formal capitulation on 5 October 1944. Warsaw had become "a city of ruins" during Operation *Tempest.* The Germans gradually regained control of the city district by district until only the central district was defended by the Poles. Withdrawal through the sewers became imperative. On 1 October, Lieutenant General Tadeusz Bór-Komorowski, Commander of the Polish Home Army, decided to surrender.

Right
Negotiations over capitulation and the treatment of captured insurgents was conducted between representatives of the German command and Countess Tarnowska from the Red Cross.

Right
The capitulation agreement recognized the Warsaw insurgents as combatants. The capital was to be totally evacuated, a move wholly unprecedented, condemning several hundred thousands of its inhabitants to privation, homelessness and deportation. More than 17,000 insurgents were taken prisoner, including 922 officers and 2,000 women, some of whom are shown here. A further 5,000 wounded combatants were in hospitals.

Left
Assault crossing of the Vistula. Brigadier-General Zygmunt Berling, commander of the First Polish Army had made an assault crossing of the Vistula to bring Polish units on to the western bank, where the Red Army was ensconced. Great controversy surrounded the attitude of Stalin and the passivity of the Red Army during the Warsaw rising. Rokossovskii had earlier advised Stalin that his Front could not liberate Warsaw. He therefore ordered the evacuation of Polish troops from the western bank bridgeheads.

FINLAND ELIMINATED

Knocking Finland out of the war was high on the list of Soviet priorities. To this end, the *Stavka* committed the Leningrad and Karelian Fronts: half-a-million men, 41 rifle divisions and over 800 tanks. To break through the Karelian Isthmus, thence to Vyborg, the Soviet command massed artillery and almost 500 tanks. The Soviet invasion of Estonia had already illuminated the perilous plight of the Finns, and the fall of Vyborg on 20 June produced a critical situation. The Finns, reserves exhausted, sought an armistice on 25 August. Moscow demanded an absolute break with Germany and withdrawal of all German troops.

Right
The Red Army pounded the Finns into asking for an armistice. The collapse of German Army Group North in the Baltic, and the threat to Riga, made Finnish submission inevitable. The terms of the Soviet–Finnish armistice decreed that all German troops withdraw from Finland. Colonel General Lothar Rendulic, commander of the German Twentieth Mountain Army, had already made withdrawal preparations.

Above

In October 1944, the Red Army launched its
last operation in the north, the Petsamo-Kirkenes
operation. The harsh terrain and weather conditions
made life difficult for these Karelian Front machine-gunners.
Marshal Meretskov, Karelian Front commander,
aimed his attack at the German Nineteenth Mountain Corps.

Left

With the fall of Vyborg on
20 June 1944, warning
lights flashed for the Finns.
The following day Marshal
Meretskov's Karelian Front
launched another massive
and sustained offensive
against the Finns in the
Karelian Isthmus.
Two Soviet armies, 7th
and 32nd, were committed.
A thrust also developed from
Medvezhegorsk to cut off
the Finnish "Olonets Group".
Impressed by the strength
of the Medvezhegorsk
fortifications, seen here,
Marshall Meretskov
flew to Moscow to
seek reinforcements.

Left
By the end of October, the Red Army had reached the northern frontier of Finland and was poised to push into northern Norway. German rear-guard actions, supported by artillery, held up the Soviet advance. This German rear-guard unit is preparing a bridge for demolition while withdrawing into Norway.

Below
The closing phase of the Petsamo-Kirkenes operation was a race along the northern coast of Norway. Here, local Norwegians greet Red Army soldiers on their appearance at Kirkenes in November 1944.

TRAPPING ARMY GROUP NORTH

During the autumn of 1944, the entire German northern flank became endangered. Soviet armies had already penetrated the gap between German Army Groups Centre and North. In mid-September, the Soviet armies resumed their advance toward the Baltic and Riga, bringing German Army Group North to the edge of collapse and forcing it to retreat into the Courland peninsula. With Army Group North bottled up, the *Stavka* now turned on the Third Panzer Army, which was defending the East Prussian border and German territory. Chernyakhovskii's Soviet 3rd Belorussian Front was ordered to strike into East Prussia and on 17 October, the 11th Guards Army crossed the East Prussian frontier.

Right
The 16th Lithuanian Rifle Division digging in. Following the defeat of Army Group Centre in July, the Red Army advanced with great speed into the Baltic States, penetrating eastern Latvia, Lithuania and Vilno (Vilnius).

Below
The 16th Lithuanian Rifle Division crossing a river during the Siauliai (Shauliya) operation.

Left
Soviet infantry in action
at Siauliai. The Soviet
drive for Siauliai had come
as an unpleasant surprise
to the German command.
Once it was captured,
Soviet armies were pointing
straight at the flank and
rear of Army Group
North and a catastrophic
situation appeared to
be in the making.

Below
Formation of an Estonian
tank brigade. At the end
of July 1944, Soviet
troops captured Narva,
"the gateway to Estonia".
By the end of September,
Marshal Leonid Govorov's
Leningrad Front had cleared
German forces from Estonia,
except in the Baltic islands.

Above
Soviet signal troops, street
fighting in Tartu, Estonia. At the
end of August the *Stavka* issued
orders to prepare a major
offensive to clear the Baltic states,
above all to capture Riga.
Marshal Govorov had taken over
the "Tartu sector", the prelude to
a drive on Tallinn.

Right
More retribution and possibly
summary execution:
the NKVD guard on the
left has his personal weapon at
the ready. The Baltic
states furnished auxiliary police
units to serve with the German
Army and volunteers to the SS.
When captured, these men were
usually subject to summary justice.

Left
Party officials and German
officers inspect East
Prussia's fortifications on
28 August. All too soon
they would be put to the
test. A week earlier,
Red Army units had begun
to arrive at the frontier
with East Prussia. Units
of the 3rd Belorussian Front,
commanded by General
Ivan Chernyakhovskii,
were skirting the frontier
line with East Prussia;
ahead of them lay formidable
fixed German defences.

THE BALKAN THRUST

Before a shot was fired, German armies in Rumania faced catastrophe, caught between the Russians eager to attack them and Rumanians eager to betray them. On 20 August, two Soviet Fronts launched the Jassy-Kishinev offensive, destroying Rumanian divisions and trapping five German corps. Then came 23 August 1944, one of the decisive days of the war. A coup in Bucharest ended Rumania's partnership with Germany. King Michael surrendered unconditionally to the Allies. Ahead of the Red Army lay the Hungarian plains, the road to Yugoslavia and Bulgaria and the gateway to Czechoslovakia and Austria. The entire German defensive system in the southeastern theatre was facing collapse.

Left
At 1000 hours on the morning of 31 August, the Red Army entered Bucharest. Orders specified that entry into the Rumanian capital would be made in "proper style … organized and disciplined, the infantry with bands playing, divisional and regimental commanders on horseback".

Right
Late in August 1944, Soviet columns fanned out and sped into the central districts of Rumania. These units making a river crossing are part of Marshal Malinovskii's strengthening of his forces on the right flank in the direction of the Carpathians. Axis forces were in continuous retreat across the Carpathians.

Left
These Cossacks under the command of Guards Captain Radugin are on the move through Western Rumania.

Right
Mine clearing on a Rumanian mountain road. Red Army sappers' tasks were fully recognized as dangerous. As Soviet soldiers grimly put it, "our sappers never make more than one mistake". This mine-detecting system cleverly attaches the detector to the rifle barrel, placing greater distance between the sapper and any mine. The senior soldier with the detector evidently has a gallantry award.

Below

A Soviet pilot receives a rapturous reception in Yugoslavia. On 6 September, Red Army troops had liberated the first few yards of Yugoslav territory. Tito and his partisans now realized that it was time to discuss the terms of Red Army entry with the Soviet command, even with Stalin himself.

Above

Two dispirited Rumanians. Marshal Antonescu had already confessed that the army was slipping out of his control. He could not blame the troops for not fighting energetically against the Russians. On 23 August 1944 the front was shattered, Russian tanks pouring through a 60-mile (96-kilometre) gap. The position of King Michael assumed extraordinary importance. In place of the Antonescus, King Michael established his own government, a non-political figure, General Sanatescu, representing the armed forces.

Left
The Red Army crossed the Bulgarian frontier on the morning of 8 September. The next day, Soviet troops were ordered to suspend military operations – the pro-Soviet Bulgarian "Fatherland Front" had seized power in Bulgaria and the war was at an end. Crowds such as these in Lovech prepared to greet the Red Army. In Silistra, the townspeople turned out in their best clothes and the fire brigade hosed down the streets for the Red Army procession.

Above
A "son of the regiment" wearing the
Red Star for bravery, surrounded by his
admirers. "Sons of the regiment" were
orphans adopted by Soviet regiments,
and were looked after like the soldiers'
own sons. They lived with the soldiers
and fought alongside them in front-line
actions. After the war, they found it
difficult to adjust to civilian life, the
company of other children and to
children's activities.

BUDAPEST: THE NIGHTMARE ASSAULT

Once Belgrade was liberated, Soviet tanks crossed temporary bridges over the Danube and drove northward into Hungary and the battle for Budapest. German troops had already occupied Hungary in March, although they could not block a Soviet advance beyond the Carpathians or eliminate the threat to Budapest. In Moscow, the Hungarians sought an armistice but the Germans pre-empted them with a coup, forestalling any Rumanian-type "treachery". On 28 October, the *Stavka* ordered a frontal attack on Budapest, aiming to capture it with "relatively small forces". But the mere five days Stalin had allotted for the capture of Budapest eventually stretched to become five horror-laden months.

Right
German tanks such as these made a menacing show in Budapest, where the balance of power was in question. The Hungarians sent a delegation to Moscow, which arrived on 1 October, seeking an armistice with the Soviet Union. The Germans already suspected a Hungarian withdrawal from the war and fanatically pro-Nazi Hungarians stood by to seize power – following a coup, a hoodlum government ruled Hungary, stiffened with German troops. The road to the Hungarian capital was now barred to the Russians.

Below
Soviet tanks on the move. Stalin wanted Budapest and he wanted it within hours. Soviet tanks had reached the suburbs of Budapest on 4 November but could not break into the capital. A second attack opened on 11 November, but failed to capture the city, which was about to suffer the ordeal of a terrible siege: bombardment, fire, killing, murder and rape.

1945

JOY AND SORROW

On 16 December 1944, as Stalin prepared the Red Army's final assault on the Third Reich, Hitler launched a devastating surprise attack in the west: the Ardennes offensive. Three German armies, with 25 divisions, swept across a 70-mile (112-kilometre) front held by only a handful of American divisions. German tanks were only three miles (five kilometres) from the River Meuse on Christmas Day.

In the east, a momentary calm had settled on the Vistula, and further north there was an operational pause necessary to resupply those Fronts assigned to the forthcoming offensive. But far to the south, in Hungary, savage fighting for Budapest raged night and day. For one of the mightiest strategic operations of the war, the massive Soviet thrust into the Reich along the Warsaw–Berlin axis, the Soviet command had assembled an appropriate force. The two Fronts involved, Zhukov's 1st Belorussian and Konev's 1st Ukrainian, mustered two-and-a-half million men, 10 armies, 163 rifle divisions, 6,500 tanks and 4,772 aircraft. The objective of the Vistula–Oder operation was to advance the Red Army 300 miles (480 kilometres) from its start line on the middle Vistula to the River Oder. This strategic assault on Germany included an attack in the direction of Königsberg and a thrust to the Baltic near Danzig. East Prussia would be sealed off from the rest of Germany. For the four major breakthrough operations the Soviet command concentrated 30 field armies, five tank armies and four air armies.

On 6 January 1945, Churchill asked Stalin "whether we can count on a major Russian offensive on the Vistula front" in order to relieve German pressure in the west. Stalin was only too pleased to oblige.

Konev attacked on 12 January, Zhukov two days later. Within six days the Red Army had accomplished a giant breakthrough extending from East Prussia to the Carpathian foothills.

Marshal Zhukov achieved tactical surprise from the outset. A pulverizing artillery barrage lasted for 25 minutes, forward battalions moved out of the Magnuszew bridgehead on the Vistula. By the evening of the first day of operations Russian tanks were driving at will as much as 20 miles (32 kilometres) beyond the breakthrough line.

The secondary attack from the Pulawy bridgehead achieved even greater success. Marshal Koniev aimed one massive blow directed along the Radom-Breslau axis. Soviet armies swept westwards, overrunning or by-passing Fourth Panzer and Ninth Army. Warsaw had already been enveloped from the north and south-west. The task of breaking into the city was rightly assigned to 1st Polish Army (1st Belorussian Front). By noon on 17 January, Polish divisions had liberated their own capital.

At the end of January, with Soviet armies now drawn up to and massed along the Oder, the capture of Berlin, a mere 48 miles (77 kilometres) from Zhukov's Küstrin bridgehead, appeared quite feasible. The General Staff had already plotted the city's capture on its operations map. On 26 January, Zhukov submitted detailed plans for a final, all-out high-speed offensive to capture Berlin. Konev's plan quickly followed. However, with the "Big Three" Yalta conference almost upon him, dangers on the flanks, shortages of munitions and lack of air support, Stalin called a temporary halt on the Berlin axis: no taking Berlin "off the march", no unnecessary risks.

The Yalta conference ended with a show of unanimity. Stalin held out the prospect of collaboration, as he gained his prime objective: the establishment of a pro-Soviet government in Poland. The Soviet Union agreed to enter the war against Japan after the defeat of Germany in return for restoration to Russia of those "historic rights violated by the treacherous attack of Japan in 1904".

This was for the future; on the morrow of the Yalta conference the Red Army faced a sudden, severe crisis in western Hungary. The battle for Budapest had finally ended in a ghastly welter of killing and destruction, but Hitler was determined to recapture the Hungarian capital and recover eastern Hungary. Undismayed by Soviet armies piling up on the Oder in late January, Hitler decided to transfer the Sixth SS Panzer Army, recently withdrawn from the Ardennes, to Hungary. The Soviet command, meanwhile, was planning the destruction of Army Group South, the complete liberation of Hungary, occupation of Vienna and a sweep toward southern Germany, cutting off German forces in Yugoslavia and forcing speedier German capitulation in northern Italy. The offensive operation was timed for 15 March 1945.

The SS struck first on 17 February. After a month of heavy fighting, the German assault slowed to a halt, tanks destroyed or marooned in low-lying ground. Thousands of German soldiers died in this nightmare as a powerful Soviet counter-offensive rolled over them, driving on to the Austrian frontier. German resistance in Hungary was at an end. The Red Army was poised to strike Vienna from two directions. On 1 April, the *Stavka* issued revised orders for the speedy capture of the Austrian capital. Further north, Zhukov's armies had halted before Berlin, a mere 35 miles (56 kilometres) away from the bridgeheads on the Oder river.

On 1 March, to the astonishment of the German command, Zhukov's tanks streaked northward, not westward, the detached armour committed to removing the danger to Zhukov's exposed right flank. This high-speed offensive was aimed at the Baltic, clearing western Pomerania and investing the western bank of the Oder. Both Zhukov and Rokossovskii raced for the Baltic. Gdynia fell first, followed by Danzig. Further south, Zhukov's arch-rival Konev was also poised along the Berlin axis, renewing his offensive to occupy western Silesia, to close on the Neisse river and bring his 1st Ukrainian Front fully abreast of Zhukov's 1st Belorussian. At the end of March, Upper Silesia was in

Soviet hands and Breslau was completely sealed off. There could be no German recovery.

The time was fast approaching to co-ordinate the operations of Anglo–American and Soviet armies advancing into Germany from west and east respectively. To this end, General Eisenhower, Supreme Allied Commander, addressed Stalin directly on 26 March 1945, ruling out any direct Anglo–American advance on Berlin. After the destruction of German forces in the Ruhr encirclement, the Allied offensive was to be in the direction of Erfurt–Leipzig–Dresden. The German defence would be split wide open once Allied forces linked up with the Red Army.

What caused consternation in London brought Stalin immediate satisfaction. He agreed with the proposal to link up in the Leipzig–Dresden area. The Red Army was to launch its main attack along that axis. Stalin conceded that "Berlin has lost its former strategic importance", hence the Red Army would commit only secondary forces toward that objective. The Soviet command planned to launch its offensive in the second half of May. On the day he sent this reply to General Eisenhower, 1 April, Stalin assembled an urgent command conference to finalize all plans and complete preparations for a gigantic Soviet offensive aimed precisely at the very heart of Berlin. This huge operation would be launched no later than 16 April and executed in the space of 12–15 days.

Stalin's suspicions had already been aroused over damaging misleading intelligence emanating from certain sources. In the event that the Eisenhower telegram was disinformation to conceal the real Allied plans, then Stalin responded in the same coin. He was, in fact, fully persuaded that the Red Army was now committed to "the race for Berlin" and he was determined that the Russians would win.

Stalin's command conference on 1 April reviewed the main operational plan for the capture of Berlin. Konev promised that the Red Army would be the first to take Berlin. Zhukov tersely reported that his Front was ready, poised to take Berlin. Three Fronts, supported by Soviet bombers, would pierce German defences by striking along several axes, cut the German Berlin grouping into isolated elements, destroy them and then seize Berlin. Between the 12th and 15th day of operations, Soviet assault forces should reach the Elbe and link up with Anglo–American armies. Given the extreme urgency, Fronts were given only 12–14 days in which to prepare. Zhukov was to launch his main attack from the Küstrin bridgehead; Konev was committed to destroying the Fourth Panzer Army to the south of Berlin, then to drive north and northwest to reach the River Elbe.

This provoked serious disagreement. Konev appeared to have been completely shut out of the Berlin operation. He now argued fiercely in favour of allowing his tank armies to aim directly at Berlin's southwestern suburbs. Only Stalin could decide this question. He settled on a cunning compromise. He eradicated the boundary line between Fronts, giving Konev an opportunity – "Whoever breaks in first, let him take Berlin". He advised Konev to work out an "operational variant" that allowed him to use his tank armies to attack Berlin from the south once he had broken through the German defences. In effect, Zhukov and Konev must now race each other into Berlin. Even more bizarre was the exclusion of Rokossovskii from this crucial command conference. Rokossovskii's 2nd Belorussian Front would not participate directly in the capture of Berlin, rather attacking in a westerly direction toward Berlin, securing the Soviet offensive to the north.

During the final preparation across an arc of 230 miles (370 kilometres) for the assault on Berlin, Soviet armies finally battered their way into Königsberg and fought their way into Vienna. The Soviet advance west of Vienna outflanked the German Army group defending Czechoslovakia, preparing the way for a Soviet drive on Prague. Hitler's "intuition" correctly divined Prague as a Soviet objective but failed, perhaps subconsciously, to identify Berlin as the immediate target. On 11 April, American tanks reached the Elbe, pushing on to under 50 miles (80 kilometres) from Berlin, but within hours the US Ninth Army was halted, the final push to Berlin abandoned.

Five days later, the Soviet attack opened. Konev made rapid progress over the River Neisse, speedily implanting himself within the breakthrough zone to Berlin. Zhukov's massive attack faltered, impaled on the Seelow Heights. Stalin told Konev, "Turn your tank armies on Berlin." At the price of heavy losses, Zhukov battered his way ahead.

On 20 April, Zhukov's guns opened fire directly on Berlin. Konev's tanks were racing to Berlin from the south. Stalin was nervous. "Will the Americans and English get to Berlin before us?" To forestall this possibility, Soviet infantry armies were ordered to outflank Berlin to the north and south, driving to the Elbe and sealing off Berlin from the Allies. On 21 April, Zhukov's tanks were fighting in Berlin's northern suburbs, Konev's in the southern suburbs. Two days later, Stalin set a fresh boundary between Zhukov and Konev, slicing right through Berlin and disbarring Konev, by a mere 100 yards (90 metres) or so, from any attempt to take the greatest prize of all, the Reichstag. The palm would go to Zhukov, "conqueror of Berlin", exactly what Stalin had decided in November 1944. The total encirclement of Berlin was complete on 25 April, the day Soviet and American troops linked up on the Elbe, cutting Germany into two isolated segments, north and south. Half a million Soviet troops, 12,700 guns, 21,000 Katyusha multiple-rocket launchers and 1,500 tanks now swarmed for the final assault on Berlin's blazing, shell-shattered centre. Soviet guns hammered away relentlessly on Germany's capital.

Where the Red Army did not as yet rampage, the SS hunted down deserters. Only a strip of Berlin remained to the defenders. On the evening of 30 April, the Red Army Victory Banner hung high over the Reichstag. Hitler was already dead by his own hand. At 3 p.m. on 2 May 1945, Soviet guns ceased fire in Berlin. In the course of the capture of Berlin, the drive to the Elbe and the Baltic the Red Army destroyed 70 German infantry divisions and 12 Panzer divisions, captured 1,500 tanks and took 480,000 prisoners. Berlin cost the Red Army 325,475 casualties, 2,156 tanks and 527 aircraft.

Stalin had not finished racing the Anglo–American armies. In the north, Rokossovskii was racing the British Army into Lübeck. Prague seemed to be still within the reach of the Western allies. The American Third Army was already across the Czechoslovak frontier. Wasting neither time nor words, Stalin ordered Konev to disengage from Berlin and mount an operation to take Prague. Offers of American assistance were categorically refused. Konev's tank armies sped south, while two Soviet Fronts closed on Prague from the east. On 8 May 1945, Field Marshal Keitel signed Germany's act of capitulation in Berlin, but in Czechoslovakia Field Marshal Schörner still resisted. Konev gave all German units in western Czechoslovakia three hours to surrender. Early on 9 May, his tanks reached Prague. Shortly after noon they linked up with Malinovskii's tanks advancing from the east.

The war on the Eastern Front had ended.

TO THE ODER, TO BERLIN

In mid-January 1945, the Red Army launched the Vistula–Oder Operation, a giant offensive involving four Fronts: Konev's 1st Ukrainian, Chernyakhovskii's 3rd Belorussian, Zhukov's 1st Belorussian and Rokossovskii's 2nd Belorussian. The main effort was to be made along the Warsaw–Berlin axis, where Zhukov unleashed a savage, relentless offensive. On 17 January, Warsaw was cleared of German troops. By 20 January, a gigantic Soviet breakthrough had ripped an enormous 350-mile (560-kilometre) gap in the German front, stretching from East Prussia to the foothills of the Carpathians. The German defensive system had been either destroyed or bypassed and the Red Army had already reached the Oder river.

Above
The Red Army on the Oder. General Semen Bogdanov's 2nd Guards Tank Army reached the Oder river at 10 a.m. on the morning of 31 January. The following day, more Soviet armour drew up in strength. Fighting went on in the eastern approaches to Küstrin, the confluence of the Oder and the Warhte rivers.

Left
The Red Army at the Oder bridgeheads. On 2 February, General Chuikov's 4th Guards Corps launched an assault to seize a bridgehead on the western bank, attacking Kietz in the southern suburbs of Küstrin. Thin ice, combined with German air attacks and lack of heavy bridging equipment, prevented the Red Army from transferring guns and tanks across the Oder.

Right
In December 1944, Hitler created the Deutscher Volkssturm, the German home defence force, seen here in field defences in the region of Frankfurt–an–der–Oder. War production had priority and training in anti-tank and infantry tactics was confined to four hours on Sundays. With the Red Army now on German territory, Volkssturm units were deployed in the front line.

THE REDUCTION OF BUDAPEST

On 5 December 1944, Malinovskii's 2nd Ukrainian Front renewed its assault on Budapest in the first stage of an operation to encircle the Hungarian capital. Behind the lines in Soviet-occupied Hungary, Stalin hurried to establish a new pro-Soviet Hungarian government. Determined to hold Budapest, Hitler ordered a counter-attack west and south of the city, where

Malinovskii's assault units were already fighting. Soviet guns were ranged on Buda and Pest on either bank of the Danube and Soviet bombers pounded strong points.

On 3 February 1945, Malinovskii made "a fresh decisive effort". Ten days later, fighting ceased – the battle for Budapest had ended, but the fight for Hungary was not yet over.

Right
Soviet Katyusha multiple-rocket launchers firing on Budapest suburbs. At New Year, Red Army detachments were already in the outer suburbs. From here, on the easterly bank of the Danube, Marshal Malinovskii proposed to mount his main assault on the city. The German garrison worked frenziedly to fit out Budapest for a siege.

Left
A Soviet IL-2 Shturmovik ground-attack aircraft over Budapest. Factories had already been heavily attacked by Soviet aircraft and German supplies fell off drastically. Artillery ammunition was running short and fuel supplies were almost expended, leaving immobilized tanks to fire off the last of their ammunition from fixed-gun positions. German Ju-52s used the grass track of the race course to bring in ammunition and take out the wounded.

Left

A Red Army observation post high up in a clock tower looking for German positions. Soviet assault squads could not advance along streets that were swept by German guns. Instead, they closed on their objectives by passing through holes blown in walls by heavy guns, which blasted passages for infantry to reduce enemy positions.

Left

Soviet infantry street-fighting in Budapest. In mid-January, the Soviet "Budapest operational group", comprising the 30th Rifle, 18th Guards and 7th Rumanian Corps, reported that the whole of Pest was clear of the enemy. Pest had almost ceased to exist: it was now a mass of flaming wreckage, its streets reduced to total ruins, its buildings burned out. The rationing system for the civilian population had broken down completely and German soldiers' rations amounted to 3oz (90g) of bread a day.

Above
A gunboat of the Danube
Flotilla, commanded by Rear
Admiral Georgii Kholostyakov.
These gunboats provided
fire support to Soviet infantry
in the assault on Budapest.
They also transported troops,
ammunition and supplies
and carried out mine-
sweeping. Their fire-power
was supplied by bolting
a tank turret to the deck.

THE DEATH CAMPS: AUSCHWITZ 1945

At the end of January 1945, "everything turned out as planned" on Marshal Konev's left flank, which was committed to capturing the Silesian industrial region. On the southern encircling drive, the 59th and 60th Armies were advancing on Rybnik. In the course of this manoeuvre, riflemen from General Kurochkin's 60th Army stumbled on the German death camp at Auschwitz (Oswiencim) and discovered how its industrial processes had been hideously perverted for the purposes of mass extermination. They found the gas chambers and crematoria, the "giant's staircase" of piled suitcases, the ghastly mountain of ten tons of women's hair, and grotesque pyramids of dentures and spectacles from those consigned to death.

Right
The death camp Auschwitz was liberated in 1945. The slogan above the gates, *"Arbeit macht frei"* (Labour liberates) was really Reich Justice Minister Otto Thierack's *"Vernichtung durch Arbeit"* (Destruction through labour) applied "to liberate the German people from the Poles, Russians, Jews and Gypsies".

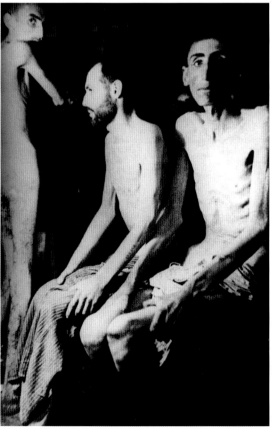

Left
In a world of unimaginable horror, death camp inmates were beaten, starved, tortured, deliberately degraded and forced to punitive hard labour, where SS guards made sport of them. Auschwitz was the largest concentration camp, the largest labour camp and the largest death factory in the Nazi system.

Left
A young Russian woman deported and subjected to forced labour working in a Nazi war factory, identified as such by the label OST – for *Ostarbeiterin* – on her overall. She was but one of the millions of deportees shipped into Germany in cattle trucks. By the end of 1944, more than two million Soviet citizens had been deported to Germany to provide forced labour. From Belorussia alone, 330,000 individuals had been deported to Germany to work in factories, on the land and as domestic servants.

Right
Homeward bound! The repatriation of forced labourers from Germany to the Soviet Union, where an uncertain future awaited them. Not all elected to return.

"THE BIG THREE" CONVENE: YALTA 1945

The Crimean Conference convened at Yalta between 4 and 11 February 1945. Yalta tested the Grand Alliance to its limits. Behind the spirit of Yalta lay the reality of extensive Soviet military victories. A key issue was whether or not Stalin would choose collaboration. He indicated that he would pursue co-operation, subject to recognition of Russia's rights. He gained his prime objective, establishment of a pro-Soviet government in Poland, and was pleased with the de-Nazification proposals for Germany, although he was denied full satisfaction over reparations. Russia would enter the war against Japan three months after Germany's defeat. Agreement at Yalta there was, but there were also hidden, dangerous, even fatal ambiguities.

Right
Soviet Foreign Minister Molotov and British Foreign Secretary Eden at Yalta signing the Declaration on Liberated Europe. Stalin had unbounded enthusiasm for the Declaration because it did not alter his hold on Eastern Europe. At the time, Yalta was hailed as "the high tide of Big Three unity". Only later was it described as a "surrender to Stalin".

Left
Seated left to right: Prime Minister Churchill, President Roosevelt and Marshal Stalin. It is an obviously weary and sick Roosevelt. Many attributed his supposed giving in to Stalin's wiles to his failing strength. As Soviet armies advanced deep into east-central Europe, it was clear that neither Britain nor the United States could negotiate from a position of strength. In less than two months, President Roosevelt was dead.

"THE LAIR OF THE FASCIST BEAST": EAST PRUSSIA

The 3rd Belorussian Front closed on East Prussia's eastern frontier on 13 January, launching an offensive to destroy the German "Tilsit–Insterburg group", its final objective being Königsberg, "citadel of East Prussia". To reinforce this attack, the *Stavka* ordered Rokossovskii's 2nd Belorussian Front to complete the isolation of East Prussia. Speed, frenzy and savagery marked Rokossovskii's advance into the "lair of the Fascist beast", as East Prussia became completely encircled.

The formidable fortress of Königsberg was also cut off, apparently about to fall speedily, yet it took weeks of ferocious fighting and horrendous human loss before "Festung Königsberg" was reduced.

Left
East Prussia proved a tough nut to crack. These Soviet soldiers are inspecting a demolished German fortification, fixed and formidable defences that had to be blown out of the ground. Marshal Rokossovskii considered the East Prussian campaign ill-conceived. It meant throwing his armies against the fortified and well-defended eastern and southeastern areas, rather than attacking from south to north.

Left
This refugee column in East Prussia has been lucky so far. These columns, which included allied prisoners of war and slave labourers, trudged out of East Prussia on foot or in farm carts; some were charged down or crushed into a bloody smear of humans and horses by juggernaut Soviet tank columns racing ahead with assault infantry atop the T-34s.

Right
Soviet tanks from a Guards
unit force the River Warthe.

Left
Soviet tanks made no
allowance for either friend
or foe as they raced toward
Königsberg. Whether the
obstructions on the road
were refugees or unburied
German dead made little
or no difference. Looking
impassively at what lay
about them on the road,
the crew of this horse-drawn
anti-tank gun push on.

Left

"We will hold Königsberg," announces the placard in a German gun position. Three lines of defences ringed Königsberg, comprising powerful forts, innumerable pill-boxes, well-constructed fortified buildings and countless other obstacles. General Chernyakhovskii opened the Soviet assault on 13 January, an operation that was not speedily concluded.

Right

The scene in Königsberg the day it was taken by the Soviet Army, 9 April 1945. General Chernyakhovskii had been killed in action earlier. Marshal Vasilevskii assumed command of the 3rd Belorussian Front. He proceeded to prepare Operation *Samland*, the final assault. The preliminary bombardment of Königsberg began early in April and involved four armies made up of 137,250 men massively reinforced with 5,000 guns, 538 tanks and 2,444 aircraft. Almost half the artillery strength consisted of large-calibre guns.

Left
Destroyed German equipment in Königsberg. General O. Lasch, commander of "Festung Königsberg", capitulated on 9 April. On Hitler's orders, he was sentenced to death and his family arrested. The Red Army claimed 42,000 Germans killed and 92,000 prisoners. The civilians suffered cruelly, trapped without any means of escape, a situation deliberately planned by East Prussia's Gauleiter. A quarter of the populace, 25,000 people, perished under the constant bombardment and ferocious street fighting.

Right
Breslau, 8 May 1945, the day Germany capitulated. The Red Army had entered the city the day before. The German garrison of 35,000 men, reinforced by civilian volunteers, had resisted repeated Soviet attacks. The bulk of the population had been forcibly evacuated by the Nazis. Many were killed in the Royal Air Force attack on Dresden.

Left
Street fighting in "Festung Breslau", chief city of Silesia. Breslau, yet another Hitler fortress, was already encircled by 15 February. Two German infantry divisions were ordered to break out, leaving only the 609th to hold the fortress, supplemented by SS units, the Luftwaffe and Volkssturm personnel. Konev deliberately bypassed Breslau, leaving Lieutenant General Vladimir Gluzdovskii's small 6th Army to lay siege to Breslau. Repeated attempts to storm the city failed.

THE RED DANUBE: VIENNA

In mid-February, the *Stavka* aimed to destroy German Army Group South. Striking from the western bank of the Danube, Soviet forces would move on Brno, Vienna and Graz, clear Hungary and deprive Germany of the Nagykanizsa oil field. But Hitler struck first, using the Sixth Army and Sixth SS Panzer Army, the latter transferring from the west, in a counter-offensive to restore German fortunes in Hungary. In late March, Tolbukhin's 3rd Ukrainian Front successfully counter-attacked, encircling Sixth Panzer and preparing to close on Vienna. The Soviet assault, joined by Malinovskii's 2nd Ukrainian Front, opened on 6 April. After fiercely fought street battles between the Soviets and German rearguards, Vienna was pronounced clear on 13 April.

Above
Soviet self-propelled guns in the streets of suburban Vienna. The Soviet assault on the city had opened on the morning of 6 April with 4th Guards Army attacking the eastern and southeastern sectors of the city. General Andrei Kravchenko's 6th Guards Tank Army received orders to strike northward to cut German escape routes.

Right
By 8 April, fighting had moved closer to the centre of Vienna, where these Soviet machine-gunners are deployed. The Arsenal and the South and East Stations were in Russian hands and panic and disorder were spreading. Attempts to set up a hasty defence to the west of Vienna had failed.

Left
Soviet mortar crews passing the Austrian Parliament building. To cover the withdrawal of their tanks across the Danube, the Germans fought fierce rear-guard actions. At 1400 hours on 13 April, the Soviet command declared Vienna cleared of enemy troops.

Above

The Soviet press announced, "the Viennese are helping the Red Army …". Some, like these, applauded. Members of the Austrian resistance movement "0–5" tried to guide Soviet tanks into the centre of the city. Others took up rifles to fire at German troops. German attempts to set up strong points in houses and basements were resisted by the inhabitants.

BREAKOUT TO THE SEA

In late February, the *Stavka* ordered Zhukov and Rokossovskii to mount a joint attack on East Pomerania. Aimed in the general direction of Kolberg, the new offensive was designed to bring both the 1st and 2nd Belorussian Fronts to the Baltic coast. Once on the Baltic, Rokossovskii was to turn to seize Danzig and Gdynia, while Zhukov's right flank was charged with advancing on Kolberg, breaking out to the Baltic and clearing western Pomerania. On 25 March, Rokossovskii reached the Gulf of Danzig. Gdynia fell first. Rejecting surrender, Danzig was attacked on three sides and finally cleared of German troops on 30 March.

Above
Soviet troops reached the Gulf of Danzig at the end of March. Marshal Rokossovskii planned to split the Danzig-Gdynia fortified area in two, separating Danzig from Gdynia. The first attack was aimed at Sopot, a seaside resort, seen here during an attack by Soviet infantry.

Left
These German refugees in Danzig are fleeing to the mouth of the Vistula – others committed suicide, fearing to fall into Russian hands. The German garrison rejected the Soviet offer of surrender. The port was attacked from three sides on 26 March and German troops defended the port from building to building, calling on German warships for fire support. On 30 March, it was all over.

"WHO WILL TAKE BERLIN?"

Stalin was determined to win "the race for Berlin". Three Soviet Fronts would pierce German defences, isolate and destroy the enemy and seize the city. The Red Army would also advance to the Elbe and link up with Allied troops. More than two million men, 6,250 tanks, 41,000 guns and 7,500 aircraft were committed to this mightiest of Soviet offensives, which opened on 14–15 April. Konev made rapid progress, while Zhukov was stalled on the Seelow Heights.

Stalin now deliberately set Zhukov and Konev in competition against each other to enter Berlin with their forces. After 26 April, one week of final ferocious fighting inside Berlin left the city ablaze and in ruins.

Right
Volkssturm defenders on the streets of Berlin, April 1945. These elderly Home Guard had as their total armament a *Panzerfaust* anti-tank weapon. The *Panzerfaust* was a recoilless rocket launcher that used a hollow charge bomb, fired from a disposable tube launcher. It was carried and fired by one man. The projectile had a range of 110 yards (100 metres) and was capable of penetrating 8 inch- (20 cm-) thick armour.

Left
Soviet tanks on the streets of Berlin. On the morning of Saturday 21 April, a heavy Soviet artillery bombardment signalled to Berliners that the city was under immediate and sustained attack. Zhukov's tanks and infantry closed on the northern and northeastern suburbs, skirting *Panzerfaust* ambushes mounted by old men and schoolboys.

Left
Monster at the gates:
a Soviet "Joseph Stalin"
IS-2 heavy tank armed with
a 122-mm D-25T gun at
the Brandenburg Gate.
The size of the tank is well
illustrated by comparison with
the figure of the Soviet soldier
and the horses behind him.

Below
A typical Red Army assault
detachment passing unburied
German dead in a Berlin street.
Urgency was the order of the
day, with Zhukov's men under
orders to advance as speedily as
possible into the very centre of
Berlin. All armies organized battle
groups, with assault groups at
company strength composed of
riflemen, artillery, tanks, the
ubiquitous combat engineers and
indispensable flame-throwers for
reducing bunkers and strong
points, incinerating soldiers,
civilians, women and children.

JOY AND SORROW: **1945**

Right
Soviet Shturmovik ground-attack aircraft were part of a massive Soviet air effort totalling 7,500 aircraft in the final battle for Berlin. Shturmoviks carried out low-level attacks on German tanks and crumbling defences. In addition to the Shturmovik attacks, Soviet bombers targeted tactical objectives in the Berlin defence perimeter.

Left
T-34 tanks, hatches open, advance towards the centre of Berlin. This is a sector where the fighting has presumably died down and the inhabitants have come out to watch, like the lady on the right who, for some reason, is holding a pair of shoes.

Right
Civilian refugees at the
Landwehr Canal. The SS
had blown up a four-mile
(6.5-kilometre) tunnel that ran
beneath the Spree river and
the Landwehr Canal. The
tunnel was a railway link in
which thousands of civilians
had been sheltering. Water
flooded the area and there
was a mad scramble to
reach the higher ground. Four
hospital trains with wounded
were also trapped there.

SPLITTING HITLER'S REICH

The encirclement of Berlin was complete by 25 April. The same day, at some time in the afternoon, Soviet and United States troops linked up on the River Elbe, shattering the entire German front and slicing Hitler's Reich into two isolated segments, one to the north, the other to the south. Konev's report to Stalin on time and place was very precise:

1330 hours, 25 April, near Strehla, 58th Guards Rifle Division, 5th Guards Army made contact with reconnaissance elements of the American 69th Infantry Division, attached to 5th Corps, US First Army. Further contact was made at Torgau. The "official" US–Soviet link up was therefore celebrated at 4.40 p.m. on 25 April.

Above
The celebration of the "official" US–Soviet link up on the Elbe. The banner in Russian and English reads: "Long live the victory of the Anglo–Soviet–American military alliance over the German-Fascist occupiers". The first contact had been made by Lieutenant Albert Kotzebue of the 69th US Infantry Division and his 26-man patrol. The first Russian soldier he met was a horseman. When American and Soviet soldiers actually met, they simply stood looking at each other.

233

CAPITULATION

Toward midday on 30 April 1945, Soviet units deployed for the final assault on the Reichstag, and Soviet heavy guns began shelling at 1330 hours. Inside the Reichstag, Soviet and German assault parties stalked each other in the gloom, but at 2250 hours the Soviet Victory Banner was raised high over the building.

In the *Führerbunker*, General Weidling, the Berlin battle commandant, learned that Hitler was dead. German emissaries now sought a cease-fire to negotiate capitulation terms with the Russians, who demanded immediate and unconditional surrender. Marshal Zhukov accepted the surrender of Berlin at 0645 hours on 2 May. At 3 p.m., Soviet guns ceased fire.

Left
Hitler takes his last glimpse of the outside world. The Red Army in Berlin did not know of Hitler's whereabouts; to prevent his possible escape, the Soviet command ordered a rapid attack on the aerodrome at Tempelhof. By 26 April the runways were in Soviet hands.

Right
The squat, dark building on the left is the entrance to the *Führerbunker*. For those in the bunker, life had taken on "an aimless, dreamlike quality"; maps were spread on tables, doors left open. The Goebbels family had moved into the bunker, and Hitler paced up and down, talking to anybody who remained. No-one doubted that Hitler intended to commit suicide – and this he did.

Above
Jubilation! The Victory Banner
has flown above the Reichstag.
Captain Neustroev's battalion
rushed the building and
Sergeants Meliton Kantariya
and Mikhail Yegorov, after a
second assault on the evening
of 30 April, planted the victory
banner high over the Reichstag
at 2250 hours.

235

Right
The Reichstag, like the rest of Berlin, had been reduced to ruins. Inside the shell of the Reichstag, Soviet and German assault parties stalked each other in the gloom. Soviet rifle companies hurriedly set up a defensive system. Elsewhere in Berlin fires blazed and guns continued to fire, pounding a garrison now cut into four isolated groups.

Left
General of Artillery Helmuth Weidling, Berlin Commandant, (second left) with his staff. Weidling had realized that the situation in Berlin was hopeless. This was confirmed in the *Führerbunker*, where he met Josef Goebbels and Martin Bormann. Sworn to secrecy, Weidling was told Hitler was dead and his body was burned. Negotiations for a cease-fire and terms of capitulation were now authorized.

FROM CAPITULATION TO SURRENDER

Grossadmiral Karl Dönitz, Hitler's successor, found it difficult to comply with General Eisenhower's demands for unconditional German surrender on all fronts. Even if he did agree, he could not guarantee compliance by men on the Eastern Front, fearful of the Russians, intent on fleeing westwards. On May 6 he asked Colonel-General Alfred Jodl to present fresh German proposals at Eisenhower's headquarters at Rheims, repeating the desire to surrender to the Americans. Eisenhower insisted on unconditional surrender, though Jodl argued desperately for a German surrender to the West rather than to the Russians. Dönitz finally conceded. The "first" German surrender took place in Rheims at 0241 hours, 7 May 1945. Stalin immediately demanded a re-run, a "second" unconditional surrender to east and west alike, enacted in Berlin, with Zhukov present.

Above

This interesting photograph shows the Soviet re-enactment of the surrender of the Third Reich. Marshal Zhukov is seated directly beneath the flags. On his right is Air Chief Marshal Sir Arthur W. Tedder, on his left General Carl Spaatz. On the extreme left, on Tedder's right, sits Andrei Vyshinsky, assigned as "special adviser" to Zhukov. On the extreme right, Field Marshal Wilhelm Keitel signs "The Act of Surrender". Stalin had demanded that the formal signing of the Act of Military Surrender must take place in Berlin on 8 May in the presence of the entire "Supreme Command of the Anti-Hitler Coalition" and the German High Command.

Right
The second time around.
Two old men, sitting amid
the ruins of Berlin, stare
at defeat for the second
time, first in 1918 and
now again in 1945.

Left
Kaput! A German
officer, head in hands,
realizes that the end is
inevitable and imminent.

Above
These inhabitants of Berlin are queuing to obtain water. Berlin was a ruined city and now lacked essential services such as telephones, gas supplies, trams and the underground railway. Health services were a severe problem – the special hospitals that had been set up were crammed with the wounded. Almost half of Berlin's houses were totally destroyed and another third partly destroyed.

Above
German prisoners of war at an assembly point in Berlin. The Red Army estimated that it had destroyed no fewer than 70 German infantry divisions and 12 Panzer divisions. In Berlin itself on 2 May, Zhukov's armies took 100,000 men prisoner, Konev's 34,000. The Berlin operation cost the Red Army 304,887 men killed, wounded or missing.

Right
German civilians returning to Berlin. Civilian losses during the battle of Berlin were high. One estimate puts the total in the region of 100,000. At least 20,000 were victims of heart attacks and 6,000 or more committed suicide. The rest were probably killed by the continuous shelling, were caught up in street-fighting or died of wounds.

THE PRAGUE RISING

The citizens of Prague took to the streets on 4 May, their mass demonstrations surprising those who had been planning an organized rising. Appeals for help went out to both the Russians and the Americans. An additional appeal in Russian went to the "Vlasov Army", requesting support for the Prague rising.

Having first helped the Czechs, the "Vlasovites" again closed ranks with the SS to escape the Red Army. With unconditional German surrender on 8 May, German surrender in Prague was speedily enacted. Marshal Konev had already launched his Prague operation on 6 May. His tanks reached Prague on 9 May, linking up with Malinovskii advancing from the southeast.

Left
The citizens of Prague taking to the streets. Excited by the news of the American advance into Bohemia, the populace tore down German street signs or painted them with patriotic slogans. On 5 May, "Station Prague" broadcast a dramatic appeal, asking people to support the rising, to man barricades and block roads and avenues.

Right
Marshal Konev in Prague. On the very last day of the war, Konev's tanks had made a spectacular break-through to Prague, advancing from Saxony in the north. Travelling at breakneck speed, Soviet tanks reached Prague in the early hours of the morning of 9 May 1945. The link-up with Marshal Malinovskii occurred shortly after noon.

Left
No-one is happier than this
Soviet soldier. At 2000 hours
on 8 May, Marshal Konev
had ordered the capitulation
of all German units in western
Czechoslovakia. He allowed
the German command three
hours in which to submit.

Right
The burial of Red Army
soldiers with full military
honours in Prague. Civic
dignitaries and political
leaders are in attendance.
The Prague operation
involved the 1st, 4th and 2nd
Ukrainian Fronts. The cost to
the Red Army was 49,348
killed, wounded and missing.

REVENGE AND RETRIBUTION

General Vlasov fell into Soviet hands in Czechoslovakia in May 1945. The "Vlasovite" troops, who had first supported the rising in Prague, marched south to meet the Americans. The 1st Division was disarmed by the Americans in the Schlusselburg region, where Vlasov also arrived. The Russians were informed that the Americans would evacuate Schlusselburg and hand the town to the Red Army. Vlasov and his column left Schlusselburg hoping to enter the American zone, but were intercepted by a Soviet column. In Moscow, Vlasov and eleven others were tried for treason and hanged on 2 August 1946. Vlasov refused to confess, despite being told he would be tortured to death without trial.

Right
Lieutenant General Vlasov and his fellow officers in the dock (front row, left to right): Andrei Vlasov, G.N. Zhilenkov, G.A. Zverev, V.I. Maltsev.

Left
The accused in German uniform; left to right: Major General Georgii Zhilenkov, former Communist Party functionary and Vlasov's propaganda director; Major General G.A. Zverev, former Red Army divisional commander, appointed commander of the 2nd Division of the Russian Liberation Army; and Major General V.I. Maltsev, former Red Air Force commander in Central Asia, commander of Vlasov's air squadron.

Above
Thus Vlasov died in the Lubyanka.
There was every reason to avoid a
public "show trial". It would
immediately stir the memory of
millions of Russians in former
German-occupied territory,
reminding them of the extent of the
collaboration with the Germans.

SALUTING THE DESERVED VICTORY

Moscow celebrated the Soviet victory over Germany with the Victory Parade on 24 June 1945, notable for the appearance of Marshal Zhukov on a white charger. Stalin took the salute. The Parade was a complete review of all branches of the Soviet armed forces, with each Front represented by a "composite regiment" led by senior Soviet commanders with sabres drawn. The Victory Banner planted atop the Reichstag was flown into Moscow on 20 June for the Parade, its honour guard commanded by Guards Captain Valentin Varennikov, the Banner borne by Hero of the Soviet Union, Senior Sergeant F.A. Shkirev.

Left
A rare picture of Stalin (front row, second from right) with his commanders. Having been elevated to Marshal in 1943, Stalin now assumed the historic title of Generalissimus. On Stalin's left, Marshal Voroshilov, an old war-horse and crony; on his right, Marshal Zhukov; next to Zhukov, Marshal Vasilevskii. Front row, the two from the left are: Chief Marshal of Artillery N.N. Voronov and Marshal Budenny, yet another old war-horse.

Right
The Victory Parade in Moscow, 24 June 1945. Left-to-right: Marshal Budenny, Generalissimus Stalin and Marshal Zhukov on the Kremlin saluting stand to review the victory parade.

Left
Soviet tanks move to Red Square for the Victory Parade. The wartime "learning curve" of the Soviet tank forces was cruel and costly. The answer lay with the reorganization of Red Army mobile forces, increasing the ratio of armour to infantry. At the end of the war, the Red Army was deploying no fewer than six Tank Armies.

Above
VE–Day celebrations in Red Square, Moscow, 9 May 1945.

Below
More celebration as Muscovites dance in the streets on 9 May.

Left

Massed parade ranks
of decorated Red Army
frontoviki, front-line veterans.
Soviet infantry had carried
the brunt of the fighting on
the Eastern Front and suffered
the heaviest casualties.
The "mob of riflemen" of the
1941 rifle divisions took
time to evolve into a
trained fighting force.
After Stalingrad, Soviet rifle
divisions were supplied
with greater heavy-weapon
support, but still maintained
many men "right up front",
thus inviting heavy casualties.

Right

At the victory parade, each
Front was represented by a
composite regiment with
army commanders in the
lead, sabres drawn. Marshal
Malinovskii led the Second
Ukrainian Front, with five
army commanders in the first
rank.–The standard bearer
was Guards Lieutenant
Colonel I.M. Kovtunyak.
The riflemen are carrying
SVT-40 automatic rifles with
fixed bayonets.

Left

The Soviet Navy on parade.
The composite regiment
representing the navy was
commanded by Vice-Admiral
V.G. Fadeev. Throughout the
war, the Soviet navy operated
against enemy warships and
enemy transports, escorted
convoys, defended naval
bases and carried out
amphibious operations.
Its total wartime losses,
killed, missing and wounded,
amounted to 238,614 men.

Above

"To the soldier who is the victor, love from all the people!"
Soviet wartime poster art was especially graphic. Many posters
were works of art in their own right, the product of
distinguished Soviet artists and famous caricaturists.

Above

Captured Nazi banners.
Soldiers and sergeants form
the 1st NKVD Motor Rifle
Division. In the front rank,
left to right, are: Sergeant
F.A. Legkoshkur, Senior
Sergeant B.M. Lugovoi,
Corporal V.F. Beloshnikov,
Sergeant S.G. Kartsev.

Left

A photograph to end
with. Nikolai Voznesenskii
(centre) welcomes soldiers
returning home after the war.
Voznesenskii was one of the
main architects of the Soviet
war economy, a member of
the State Defence Committee
and was responsible for the
production of weapons and
ammunition. In 1949, he fell
foul of Stalin, was implicated
in the "Leningrad affair" and
shot. He was posthumously
"rehabilitated" in 1954.

INDEX

SELECTED READING

Adair, Paul, *Hitler's Greatest Defeat: The Collapse of Army Group Centre, June 1944*, London, 1994.

Axworthy, Mark, *Third Axis, Fourth Ally. Roumanian Armed Forces in the European War, 1941-1945*, London, 1995.

Barber, John and Harrison, Mark, *The Soviet Home Front 1941-1945: a social and economic history of the USSR in World War II*, London, 1991.

Bartov, Omer, *The Eastern Front 1941-1945, and the Barbarisation of Warfare*, London 1985.

Bedeschi, Giulio *Fronte russo: c'ero anch'io*, Vol.2, Milan 1983 Italian Army, *Armata Italiana*, in Russia.

Beevor, Antony, *Stalingrad*, London, 1998.

Chuikov, Vasilii, *The Beginning of the Road*, London, 1963. (Translation) *Nachalo puti*, Marshal Chuikov's personal account of the Stalingrad battle.

Clark, Alan, *Barbarossa the Russian-German Conflict 1941-1945*, London 1965. Reprinted 1996, 2000.

Craig, William, *Enemy at The Gates: The Battle for Stalingrad*, New York 1975.

Dallin, Alexander, *German Rule in Russia 1941-1945. A Study of Occupation Policies*, 2nd.edn. Boulder, Colorado, 1981.

Duffy, Christopher, *Red Storm on the Reich. The Russian march on Germany*, London 1991.

Erickson, John, *The Road to Stalingrad. Stalin's War with Germany*, Vol.1 London 2000 (reprint) and *The Road to Berlin*, Vol.2 London 1999 (reprint).

Etterlin, Frido M. von Senger und, *German Tanks in World War II, The Compete Illustrated History of German Armoured Vehicles 1926-1945*, London 1969.

Förster, Jürgen Ed., *Stalingrad: Ereignis-Wirkung-Symbol*, Zurich, 1992.

Garrard, John and Garrard, Carol Eds., *World War Two and the Soviet People*, London 1993.

Germany and the Second World War, Volume IV, *The Attack on the Soviet Union*. Edited by the Research Institute for Military History, Potsdam, Germany. (Trans. Ewald Osers *et. al.*) Oxford 1998. Map supplement.

Glantz, David M., and House, Jonathan M., *The Battle of Kursk*, University Press of Kansas, 1999.

Glantz, David M., and Orenstein, Harold S., (Ed., trans.), *The Battle for Kursk 1943*, The Soviet General Staff Study. London, 1999.

Glantz, David M., *Stumbling Colossus. The Red Army on the Eve of World War*, University Press of Kansas, 1998

Glantz, David M., *Zhukov's Greatest Defeat The Red Army's Epic Disaster in Operation Mars, 1942*, University Press of Kansas, 1999.

Gorodetsky, Gabriel, *Grand Delusion Stalin and the German Invasion of Russia*, Yale

Grenkevich, Leonid (Ed. David M. Glantz), *The Soviet Partisan Movement 1941-1945*, London, 1999.

Guderian, Heinz, *Panzer Leader*, London 1982 (reprint)

Hardesty, Von, *Red Phoenix. The Rise of Soviet Air Power 1941-1945*, Washington, DC, 1982.

Harrison, Mark, *Soviet Planning in Peace and War 1938-1945*, Cambridge, 1985.

Hayward, Joel S.A., *Stopped at Stalingrad The Luftwaffe and Hitler's Defeat in the East, 1942-1943*, University Press of Kansas, 1998

Heidkämper, Otto, *Vitebsk. Kampf und Untergang der 3. Panzerarmee*, Heidelberg, 1954.

Hoffmann, Joachim, *Kaukasien 1942–43 Das deutsche Heer und die Orientvölker der Sowjetunion*, Freiburg im Breisgau, 1991.

Hoth, Hermann, *Panzer Operationen*, Heidelberg, 1965.

Irving, David, *Hitler's War*, London, 1977.

Karpenko, A.V., *Obozrenie otechestvennoi bronetankovoi tekhniki (1905-1995 gg)*.

Kehrig, Manfred, *Stalingrad: Analyse und Dokumentation einer Schlacht*, Stuttgart, 1974.

Klink, E., *Das Gesetz des Handelns 'Zitadelle' 1943,*. Stuttgart 1966.

Kriegstagebuch des Oberkommandos der Wehrmacht (Wehrmachtführungsstab) 1940-1945, Ed. Hans-Adolf Jacobsen. Vols. I–IV. Frankfurt am Main, 1965.

Krivosheev, G.F., Ed., *Soviet Casualties and Combat Losses in the Twentieth Century*, London 1997. (Original: *Grif sekretnosti snyat*, Moscow 1993. Soviet manpower, equipment losses 1941–45)

Le Tissier, Tony, *Zhukov at the Oder The Decisive Battle for Berlin*, Westport, London, 1996.

Linz, Susan J., Ed., *The Impact of World War II on the Soviet Union*, Totowa, New Jersey, 1985.

Main Front: Soviet leaders look back on World War II, Foreword Marshal Sergei Sokolov. London 1987.

Malaparte, Curzio, *The Volga Rises in Europe*, (Trans. David Moore) London 1957

Manstein, Erich von, *Lost Victories*, Chicago 1958. (Original: *Verlorene Siege,* Bonn, 1955)

Minasyan, M.M., (ed.), *Great Patriotic War of the Soviet Union 1941-1945. A General Outline*, Moscow, 1974. Abridged translation, 1970 Russian edition.

Müller, Rolf-Dieter, Ueberschär, Gerd R., Eds., *Hitler's War in the East 1941-1945*, Oxford 1997.

Overy, Richard, *Russia's War*, London 1997.

Parotkin, Ivan, *The Battle of Kursk*, Moscow 1974. (Original: *Kurskaya bitva*). Senior Soviet commanders' accounts.

Parrish, Michael Ed., *Battle for Moscow,* The 1942 General Staff Study. London, 1989.

Philippi, Alfred and Heim, Ferdinand, *Der Feldzug gegen Sowjetrussland 1941 bis 1945. Ein Operativer Überblick*, Stuttgart, 1962

Poirier, Robert G., and Conner, Albert Z., *The Red Army Order of Battle in the Great Patriotic War,* Novato, Calif., 1985.

Reese, Roger R., *Stalin's Reluctant Soldiers. A Social History of the Red Army, 1925-1941*, University Press of Kansas, 1996

Reinhardt, Klaus, *Moscow: The Turning Point. The Failure of Hitler's Strategy in the winter of 1941-42*, Oxford, 1992. (Original *Die Wende vor Moskau: Das Scheitern der Strategie Hitlers im Winter 1941–42*, 1972.)

Rotundo, Louis Ed., *Battle for Stalingrad. The 1943 Soviet General Staff Study*, London, 1989.

Rzheshevsky, Oleg A., *War and Diplomacy, The Making of the Grand Alliance*, Documents from Stalin's Archives. Trans. T. Sorokina, London, 1996.

Sadarananda, Dana V., *Beyond Stalingrad Manstein and the Operations of Army Group Don*, New York, 1990.

Sajer, Guy, *The Forgotten Soldier*, Trans. Lily Emmet, London, 1971.

Salisbury, Harrison S., *The Siege of Leningrad*, London 1969.

Schofield, B.B., *The Russian Convoys*, London 1964.

Schröter, Heinz, *Stalingrad*, Trans. C. Fitzgibbon. London 1958. (Original: *Stalingrad ... bis zur letzten Patrone,* Lengerich 1953.)

Seaton, Albert, *The Russo-German War 1941-1945*, London 1971.

Shtemenko, S.M., *The Soviet General Staff at War 1941–1945.* Bks.1-2. Moscow, 1985. (Original: *Sovetskii general'nyi shtab v gody voiny*).

Shukman, Harold (ed.), *Stalin's Generals*, London 1993.

St. Petersburg, 1996. Specifications, Soviet tanks, all types.

Stalin, J., *The Great Patriotic War of the Soviet Union*, New York, 1945. Translation, 5th Russian edn., 1945. Wartime speeches.

Stalin's Correspondence with Churchill, Attlee, Roosevelt and Truman 1941-1945, Two vols. in one. London 1958. (First published USSR, 1957, reprint 1976)

Streit, Christian, *Keine Kameraden. Die Wehrmacht und die sowjetischen Kriegsgefangenen 1941-1945*, Bonn 1991 (new edition) University Press, 1999.

Velikaya Otechestvennaya voina 1941–1945 Entsiklopediya Ed. M.M. Kozlov, Moscow 1985, Soviet encyclopedia, the "Great Patriotic War".

Velikaya Otechestvennaya voina 1941–1945, Co-editors V.A. Zolotarev, G.N. Sevostyanov, Vols. 1–4, Moscow 1998-1999. The latest "official history" of the "Great Patriotic War".

Werth, Alexander, *Russia at War 1941-1945*, London 1964.

Who's Who of Prominent Germans in the USSR, London, dated 1 September 1944.

(Restricted). "All German generals captured by the Red Army, members, collaborators of the Free German Movement".

Yakovlev A.A. Academician Ed. *God 1941 Dokumenty*. Vols. 1–2. Moscow 1999. (665 documents from secret Party archives,the military, Soviet intelligence, additional section covering months June–December 1941, also Addendum, 31 documents, 1933–1940).

Zhukov, Georgii K., *The Memoirs of Marshal Zhukov*. London, 1971. (Original: *Vospominaniya i razmyshleniya*, Moscow 1969).

Ziemke, Earl F., *Stalingrad to Berlin: The German Defeat in the East*, Washington, D.C., 1968

Ziemke, *Stalingrad to Berlin: Decision in the East*, Washington, DC, 1987.

ACKNOWLEDGEMENTS

AUTHOR'S ACKNOWLEDGEMENTS

This book has its origins in the photo-archive associated with *Rodina* the Moscow-based illustrated historical journal published since 1989. *Rodina* was brought into being by the Communist Party Central Committee and the newspaper *Pravda*, inheriting part of their archives. *Rodina's* photo archive consists of 30,000 images, positive photographs, negatives and slides, the bulk devoted to the many and varied aspects of both Russian and Soviet history. The archive has been augmented by purchases from private collections as well as donations from photographers themselves.

Drawing on the *Rodina* archive, between seventy-five and eighty percent of the images presented here are unpublished. A small proportion also derives from the photo archives at Krasnogorsk. Mr. Vladimir Dolmatov, Chief Editor of *Rodina*, generously gave permission to utilize the resources of the archive. Dr. Sergei Kudryashov, Editor-in-Chief of *Rodina's* supplement, *Istochnik*, Journal of the Presidential Archive, was instrumental in researching the archives, identifying relevant images and supervising their transmission to Britain. Amina Koltsova and Andrei Oldenburger undertook the scanning, all in association with Archivist Yurii Murin.

PICTURE CREDITS

The publishers would like to thank the following sources for their kind permission to reproduce the pictures in this book:

AKG London: 8, 12 bottom, 12 top left, 12 bottom right, 13 bottom left, 13 top left, 23 top, 24, 25, 46 bottom, 46 top, 65 top, 111 bottom, 117 bottom, 124 bottom, 125 top, 137botom, 137 top, 139, 154/155, 176, 179 bottom, 180/181, 181 top right, 183, 184 bottom left, 190 bottom left, 193 bottom, 193 top, 194 top, 197 bottom, 197 top, 201bottom, 202 top, 207 top, 208, 212 bottom, 213 bottom, 213 top, 215 bottom, 215 top, 220 bottom, 222 top, 223 bottom, 224, 225 bottom, 227, 228, 229 top, 230 bottom, 232, 234 bottom, 234 top, 236 top, 238 top, 241, 242 top, Bilderdienst Suddeutscher Verlag: 26 top, Corbis: 23 bottom, Hulton Getty: 26 bottom, Imperial War Museum: 30, 31 bottom, 49 bottom, 49 top, 53 bottom, 67 bottom, 123 bottom, 160/161, 169, Private Collection: 44, 45, 48 bottom, 48 top, TRH Pictures: 54 bottom, 54 top, 123 top, 192

The remaining pictures in the book were supplied from the Rodina Archive in Moscow and the Leonid Pitersky Collection in St Petersburg, and include the work of the following photographers:

N. Asnin, L. Bernstein, A. Kapustyanskiy, N. Petrov, S. Strunnikov, V. Tarasevitch, N. Figurkin, Y. Khalip, I. Ozersky, L. Leonidov, O. Knorring, B. Sheinin, G. Petrusov, Y. Riumkin, P. Gapochka, E. Tikhonov, B. Kudoyarov, A Egorov, M. Dubnov, E. Khaldei, Y. Kanenbergas, S. Gurariy, F. Kislov, M. Redkin, G. Samsonov, V. Grebnev, V. Rudnyi, A. Shaikhet, M. Trakhman, A. Ustinov, K. Vdovenko, M. Kalashnikov, S. Loskutov, S. Shagin, V. Selivanov, G. Lipskerov, L. Kovalev, V. Fedoseev, A. Brodskiy, V. Kinelovskiy, G. Khomkhora, A. Gribovskiy, A. Sokolenko, E. Mikulin, B. Kubeev, V. Mikosha, V. Dorenskiy, V. Kondratiev, D. Fedotov, A. Velikzhanin, M. Troshkin, K. Konovalov, I. Evzerikhin.

Every effort has been made to acknowledge correctly and contact the source and/copyright holder of each picture, and Carlton Books Limited apologises for any unintentional errors or omissions which will be corrected in future editions of this book